Hell No

Hell No

The Surprising Truths
the Bible Teaches about
Death, Resurrection, and Judgment

By S. L. Miller

RESOURCE *Publications* • Eugene, Oregon

HELL NO

The Surprising Truths the Bible Teaches about Death, Resurrection, and Judgment

Copyright © 2021 S. L. Miller. All rights reserved. Except for brief quotations in critical publications or reviews, no part of this book may be reproduced in any manner without prior written permission from the publisher. Write: Permissions, Wipf and Stock Publishers, 199 W. 8th Ave., Suite 3, Eugene, OR 97401.

Resource Publications
An Imprint of Wipf and Stock Publishers
199 W. 8th Ave., Suite 3
Eugene, OR 97401

www.wipfandstock.com

PAPERBACK ISBN: 978-1-6667-0024-4
HARDCOVER ISBN: 978-1-6667-0025-1
EBOOK ISBN: 978-1-6667-0026-8

Scripture quotations marked "ESV" are from the ESV Bible® (The Holy Bible, English Standard Version®), copyright by Crossway Bibles, a publishing ministry of Good News Publishers. Used by permission. All rights reserved.

Scripture quotations marked "KJV" are taken from the Holy Bible, King James Version.

Scripture quotations marked "NASB" are taken from the New American Standard Bible®, Copyright © 1960, 1962, 1963, 1968, 1971, 1972, 1973, 1975, 1977, 1995 by The Lockman Foundation. Used by permission.

Scripture quotations marked "NIV" are taken from the Holy Bible, New International Version®, NIV®. Copyright © 1973, 1978, 1984 by Biblica, Inc.™ Used by permission of Zondervan. All rights reserved worldwide.

Scripture quotations marked "NKJV" are taken from the New King James Version. Copyright © 1982 by Thomas Nelson, Inc. Used by permission. All rights reserved.

Scripture quotations marked "NLT" are taken from the Holy Bible, New Living Translation, copyright © 1996, 2004, 2007 by Tyndale House Foundation. Used by permission of Tyndale House Publishers, Inc., Carol Stream, Illinois 60188.

Scripture quotations marked "NRSV" are taken from the New Revised Standard Version Bible, copyright 1989, Division of Christian Education of the National Council of the Churches of Christ in the United States of America. Used by permission. All rights reserved.

Table of Contents

Introduction: A Thirsty Pilgrim in Search of Truth 1
Chapter 1: God's Character—Why It Matters 11

PART 1: DEATH AND RESURRECTION
Chapter 2: The Soul and Death 25
Chapter 3: What Is the Spirit? 31
Chapter 4: The State of the Dead in the Old Testament 35
Chapter 5: But What about These OT Passages? 40
Chapter 6: The State of the Dead in the New Testament 50
Chapter 7: What Do the NT Writers Say? 57
Chapter 8: "At Home with the Lord" and "Those under the Altar" 69
Chapter 9: Jesus's Use of Gehenna 77
Chapter 10: Sleeping in Death 90
Chapter 11: Meeting the Lord in the Air 100

PART 2: JUDGMENT
Chapter 12: Born Again for Salvation 115
Chapter 13: God's Judgment upon the World 119
Chapter 14: "Wrath and Fury" and "Weeping and Gnashing of Teeth" 125
Chapter 15: Judgment—Sooner and Later 128
Chapter 16: The Dead Who "Do Not Come to Life" until the End 138
Chapter 17: The Final Judgment and the Sets of Books 144
Chapter 18: One Mind and One Voice 152

Bibliography 157
Index 159

Introduction

A Thirsty Pilgrim in Search of Truth

I ONCE HEARD A great description of how we truth-seekers should think of ourselves: as one thirsty pilgrim offering another thirsty pilgrim a cup of water. That's all I am. I'm a sixty-four-year-old woman who was raised a nominal Jew (meaning, we celebrated a couple of High Holy days and called it good). In my house, Jesus was a four-letter word (yes, his name has five letters, but you get what I mean), and Germans were still the enemy (my entire European family was gassed in Hitler's death camps). My relatives spoke a lot of Yiddish and played Canasta all the time. I was an atheist because I was raised to think that those who believed in God were stupid, uneducated, or weak. That was fine by me, for religion held no appeal to me.

When I entered my teens, my thirst for God and truth grew great. My eyes opened to the evil and injustice in the world, I couldn't fathom that life was utterly purposeless. That we evolved, and life was a blip on the screen of eternity. It terrified me to my core. Not death specifically but purposelessness. I loved the planet, and though I never thought in terms of divine intelligence or design (because, of course, intelligent people knew evolution was a proven fact), I yearned for eternity. It hurt so bad to think that this life was all there was. It made no sense. It was a complete waste.

So my heart was ripe when I was introduced to the Bible by a self-proclaimed long-haired druggie who claimed to be a prophet of God (my boyfriend's roommate). We took psychedelic drugs, read the Bible, and tried to interpret Revelation and Ezekiel to determine when the spaceships were going to come and take us away (certain the secrets lay in Ezekiel with those visions of the creatures with eyes and wheels). We sang Neil Young's song "After the Goldrush," which spoke of spaceships loaded with "chosen ones" that were set to soon fly off to a new home in the sun. We were watching the skies, waiting for those ships to take us far, far away from beautiful planet Earth that was slowly being destroyed by greedy corporations.

I was ripe, then, at age seventeen, when Jehovah's Witnesses came to my door and read Scriptures from their Bible. I thirsted for the teachings they presented and quickly devoured all their literature. A short time later I got baptized and became a "pioneer" (full-time Bible thumper). And though I went through a lot of emotional suffering during the seven years I spent in full-time ministry—after marrying an elder, I served "where the need is great" in Mississippi and at Bethel (the JW world headquarters in New York)—I learned some very important lessons for which I'm grateful.

The most important lesson was the need to go deep into Scripture to find truth. I developed intense study habits, asked the hard questions, researched Greek and Hebrew, spent endless hours in the Word searching for truth. When I left Bethel, it was during a big time of upheaval in that organization, and many, including Ray Franz—one of the governing body and nephew of perhaps the most "famous" of all JWs, Fred Franz (who had a huge hand in writing the New World Translation the JWs use)—left the organization after forty-three years of faithful service and was subsequently disfellowshipped.

This is not a diatribe or memoir about my time with the Witnesses (that's a whole other book, to be sure), but that time in my life, and especially after I got out (on the heels of contemplating suicide, due to my emotional trauma of trying to stay faithful in the cult) and engaged in correspondence with Ray Franz and others who had fled Bethel and the JWs at that time, informed how I viewed God and the Bible going forward. One of those former Bethelites told me that he went back to his Catholic roots, and there he found his peace and joy with God. He was the one who described the way true seekers on a spiritual journey should view themselves: as one thirsty pilgrim sharing a cup of water with another. We are in this wilderness together.

Fast-forward twenty-plus years: I hadn't looked at a Bible since my departure from the JWs. I spent a couple of years deep in Scripture, at first, helping others get out via some online forums. It took time to decompress, undo the brainwashing, work at my mental knots to the point where I could go on with my life somewhat resolved and content to ditch my belief in God and his Word.

Introduction

But, as Philippians 1:6 says, God wasn't done with me. He who began a good work in me was determined to see it to completion (isn't that just like God?). It's a process that continues without an expiration date.

When my current husband became a Christian in 2004, I decided I would challenge myself to delve into Scripture once again, this time to test not just what it truly taught (Was it truth? Was it consistent? What did it really teach about God?) but to test my heart. I wasn't sure I believed in God—not as the sovereign Creator of the universe. I leaned more toward the New-Agey belief that God was in me and that I was part of God in some mystical way. I felt God was best explained by Alan Watts, a follower of Buddhism, and by what Meister Eckhart said: "The eye through which I see God is the same eye with which God sees me; my eye and God's eye are one eye, one seeing, one knowing, one Love."

Yeah, ponder that one awhile!

So, I am no scholar. At the time of this writing, I'm completing a college degree in English Literary Studies. I studied art and English, built and ran a bed-and-breakfast inn while I raised two daughters, and had a pygmy goat farm. I believed that if God were to be found in the Bible, he wouldn't be found only by theologians and church fathers. With my JW background, I had learned to challenge and question everyone and every teaching (a discipline that ultimately, to their dismay, had me challenging them and finding them way off track).

Some say that since the Bible is subject to interpretation, you can find any "truth" you like in it. It's true that people the world over, throughout history, have interpreted Scripture in countless and contradicting ways. No wonder many have given up their faith and their belief in the Bible as God's inspired, inerrant Word. It's not an easy read. But when I dove back in, determined to mine its truths and see for myself what it said, I decided I would be brave and not believe what everyone else believed just because they believed it.

If there was one thing I came to understand—something I did not truly experience as a JW—it was that studying Scripture prayerfully is a one-on-one intimate undertaking with God. If I wanted to truly know him, I had to study and pray. The Bible says if we search for God—not just search but grope—he will let himself be found by us (Jer 29:13; Acts 17:27). That evokes a picture of a blind person feeling her way along, touching everything, paying close attention to every step so as not to stumble.

I have found the journey to God to be one of constant unfolding. God continuously reveals himself, and the more we draw close to him, the more he draws close to us and shows us truth in his Word. I like to say the Bible is frozen Holy Spirit. When you open it and begin reading, it thaws, and God's Spirit activates the words and meanings, allowing truth to seep into our hearts and help open our eyes. My belief is we should always adopt a humble attitude of seeker, learner, thirsty pilgrim who just wants that cup of water to revive, sustain, refresh, and, most importantly, to save. That living water that comes from Christ, that is in the Word, is there for the taking.

But What if the Bible Teaches Something Different?

But here's the challenge. If you've been taught doctrine from the Bible, and if everyone around you seems to believe all the same things, what do you do when your prayerful, personal study of the Bible reveals doctrine in opposition to those other things you were taught?

A lot of people will say that you would be crazy to think you are smarter or better equipped to interpret Scripture than the experts. I was summarily shot down by a prominent theologian who basically said I had a lot of nerve interpreting Scripture on my own instead of deferring to the church fathers who were, no doubt, chosen by God to interpret the Bible for the uneducated masses.

Certainly, many Bible scholars and theologians know their stuff and have a lot to say that is well founded. It's worth exploring Bible commentaries and listening to famous preachers.

But.

Do you just throw your hands up and think you must be foolish, rebellious, even blasphemous to think such things? For centuries the "church" claimed privilege of divine interpretation and knowledge, and anyone who dared defy them was oftentimes killed or imprisoned. Thankfully, at least at this moment in America, that's not the case. I presently have the freedom to disagree, share my cup of water, and hope it helps other pilgrims on their journey to the heart of God. Maybe someday what I've written will land me a tidy execution. I'd like to think I have the courage of my convictions. Convictions wrought from years of careful, prayerful, humble study of the Bible.

I hope you consider this foray into Scripture as not an attempt to offend, upend tradition, slam or criticize church doctrine—or condemn or

INTRODUCTION

sway you from your beliefs. I'm merely offering a cup of water, and you can drink it if you like and see if it refreshes and restores you. I believe that since a lot of things are sealed up until the end (Dan 12:4), all we can do is sincerely and honestly dig into the Bible with the sole aim of getting to know God more and more.

Some things are going to stay puzzling and vague, and while we can guess at what those passages might mean, we sometimes have to throw our hands up and know that one day the veil will be lifted and we will see everything clearly. We only know partially right now, as if looking into a foggy mirror (1 Cor 13:12). So let us work to stay humble about what we assert, and I ask your forgiveness in advance if anything I state in this book comes across with arrogance or a smug attitude of superiority.

Truth Leads to Everlasting Life

However, while some things are veiled, other things are knowable, and those are the things we need to examine, to prove to ourselves the good and perfect and acceptable will of God (Rom 12:2). My prayer is that I, and you, might know him, for to know him is to love him. And I believe when you understand what the Bible truly teaches about the soul, the spirit, death, hell, and judgment, it will help you know and love God more than you ever have. There is no need for a veil to cover our eyes on these topics, for the Scriptures, to me, are *consistently clear*.

I hope you will reserve judgment on what follows, prayerfully studying the Scriptures, their context, and the meaning of the biblical words before dissing what I share. Don't take my word for anything. This is your personal journey. It's between you and God.

I have spent many, many tearful days and nights praying for clarity, to understand truth, for wisdom (and he promises to give it generously and without reproach!—Jas 1:5), grappling with the Scriptures and trying to be open-minded and let the Holy Spirit guide me into all truth, as Jesus promised (John 16:13). I still have a long, long way to go. I don't know it all. Rather, the more I learn, the more I realize how little I know about God and his unsearchable ways (Rom 11:33).

All I have is a small cup of water. Here. Take a sip. May it refresh you and give you some strength to keep going through the wilderness. I'll meet you on the other side, where we will be like calves frolicking out of our stalls, with the sun of righteousness baking our shoulders and healing all our hurts and pain (Mal 4:2). There, we will eat and drink with Jesus in his kingdom on earth (yes, real wine and real food, as he promised—Matt 26:29). What a joyous time that will be!

Hell on Earth

The topics of death, hell, the resurrection, and judgment are not only crucial to a Christian's faith, they are crucial to having a close relationship with God. To know God is to love and trust him. If our understanding of God is flawed—even worse, grossly misunderstood—it will prevent us from loving him as deeply as he so deserves.

And, more than that, it should be every Christian's deepest heart's desire to truly know God's character and perfectly love him. The Bible says perfect love throws fear outside, but if we are falsely taught things about God that are not only fear-inspiring but unbearably horrible to consider, our love can't be made perfect. "There is no fear in love. But perfect love drives out fear, because fear has to do with punishment" (1 John 4:18 NIV). The one who fears is not made perfect in love. How can we truly love and trust a God that would do things that are utterly inconceivable to us? Horrible things that some consider not just acceptable but fair and indicative of a God who is said to be the embodiment of love (1 John 4:8)? That would be hell on earth.

Jews living during Jesus's lifetime, for the most part, weren't confused about these topics. They knew clearly what the truth was, for they were entrusted with the divine pronouncements of God (Rom 3:2). God plainly, through his Mosaic Law and the prophets he sent, revealed everything his people needed to know about the condition of death and the hope for future life. His chosen people wrote the first thirty-nine books of the Bible, and in those books, commonly called the Old Testament (OT) or Hebrew Scriptures, the entire body of writing is consistent in what it teaches about death, the condition of the dead, and what the hope is for the dead.

One important thing to keep in mind is that from the time of the last OT prophet Malachi until Jesus's arrival, God's people heard silence. Just as when the Israelites were enslaved in Egypt, four hundred years passed without God sending prophets to instruct and warn or teach his people. Understandably, the Jews of Jesus's day became infiltrated with pagan philosophies from the Romans and Greeks, and, just as in our day, these various viewpoints and teachings contaminated their belief system. There are

Introduction

instances in which Jesus addresses that, so keep that in mind as you read the gospels (and wonder at some of the strange beliefs the Jews of his day embraced).

God's Word Is Consistent

That said, the teachings in the OT are consistent. They have to be, for if one is to believe the Bible is God's holy Word, containing only truth, there can be no contradictions. In addition, the books and letters that make up the New Testament (NT) must be not only consistent within the body of that work but consistent with the Old Testament. The whole body of Scripture is either true or it's not. We base our faith on the premise that *all* Scripture is inspired of God, and it is noteworthy that the apostle Paul adds that it is useful for *reproof*, correction, and instruction (2 Tim 3:16).

We need to be humble, teachable, and correctable if we are going to grow in maturity in Christ. Our aim should be as Paul wished for his fellow believers: "And may you have the power to understand, as all God's people should, how wide, how long, how high, and how deep his love is" (Eph 3:18 NLT). I posit that no one can truly love God if he believes God tortures "immortal souls" of the wicked in a burning fire for eternity—a torture that never ends. I am actually aghast at the fact that so many Christians not only believe this but are perfectly "okay with it." They say it's God's justice, and he has the right to burn people in some macabre fire that doesn't consume or annihilate but just causes excruciating pain. Because, of course, those wicked people deserve it.

To that I say, "Seriously?" I feel sorry for anyone who tries to integrate a belief in a deeply loving and compassionate God with one who also thinks it's "just fine" to cause horrific pain to those who choose not to worship him. (And think for a moment who is usually associated with torturing "souls" in hellfire and why—and it's not our Creator.)

Just take a breath here, clear your mind of doctrine, drop your defenses, and think logically. One step at a time.

A Foundation Must Be Laid

Before you can determine anything about doctrinal truth, there are some important things that must first be understood and accepted. I call this the rule of the three C's: consistency, character, and context.

- One must acknowledge the Bible as a *consistent*, unchanging bastion of truth. Truth is fixed, inflexible, absolute. If the Bible varied on its teachings, its representation and definition of God, the promises and purposes of God, then it could not be relied upon. In simple terms, it could not be true or truth. So whenever a truth-seeker digs into Scripture, it must be with a clear belief and understanding that the Scriptures teach *one consistent truth on every and any topic.*

  This is particularly important when comparing the OT with the NT. Contrary to what many teach, Jesus did not create a new religion. He did not reveal new truth that nullified or contradicted prior revelation from God to his people. Jesus is the same yesterday, today, and tomorrow (Heb 13:8), and his truth, from Genesis 1:1 to the end of Revelation, is consistent, unchanging, wholly in agreement. Any Scriptures that *seem* to contradict the Bible's consistent teaching on a subject must be examined carefully in not just relative context but in light of the whole of Scripture.

  Jesus was a Jew. He not only followed and fulfilled the Jewish Law, he was the *Logos* through which all things were created and through whom all things will be united in heaven and earth (John 1:1–3). Anything and everything he believed and taught was in absolute harmony with all the truth God had revealed from Adam on through the prophets, until his birth on earth, and consistently true with all prophecy foretold through our day and until the end of time.

  The OT is not obsolete or wrong or incomplete. While the Mosaic Law is no longer required to be followed (Jesus fulfilled the Law, and the old covenant was subsequently replaced by the new covenant—see Heb 8:13), what the OT teaches on the topics of death, the soul, the spirit, heaven, and hell are and must be entirely and utterly consistent with what Jesus and the NT writers believed and wrote about. Any apparent difference is just that—apparent or on the surface. This is why it is so crucial that those seeking biblical truth go deep into the Word and prayerfully seek truth and not let others tell them what to believe.

- What is taught in the Bible throughout must be consistent with God's *character*. If God hates something in the OT, he hates it in the NT. God isn't going to change. Note: God makes covenants throughout history with different people and nations, and he keeps those covenants (such as with Abraham, Noah, the Israelites, etc.). Covenants sometimes

INTRODUCTION

have a proscribed length or conditions, and they can come to an end. Jesus presented "the new covenant," which replaced the old (see Jer 31:31). Prophecies are foretold and fulfilled. But, through it all, *God is always the same.*

Many refer to the "Old Testament Jehovah" as a god of anger and vengeance and suggest that God "changed," and in Jesus he is now merciful, full of grace, and forgiving. In a word: different. That is in complete opposition to Scripture. God is never-changing. He doesn't grow, learn, adjust, or mature. Yes, he chooses sometimes to change his mind, and in Scripture it plainly shows times when God pronounced judgment on a people (such as with Jonah and Nineveh), and then changed his mind and did not go through with the destruction he foretold.

But that choice to change his mind, change his decision about an action he intends, is wholly consistent with who he is. It is not flippancy or inconsistency. It is God's character to be merciful, gracious, forgiving, and patient. Repeatedly we see throughout the OT instances where God pronounced judgment and warned of destruction, only to forgive and welcome back the wayward and repentant. That is the God we know and love because we are in need of forgiveness, and God's plan of salvation is all about "while we were yet sinners, Christ died for us" (Rom 5:8 KJV). And you will see this compassionate God is in direct conflict with a god who would torture "souls" for eternity in a burning fire, to (some suppose) teach them a lesson (or because the threat is meant to deter people from sinning—more on that later). So anything gleaned from the Bible must show consistency in God's character.

- Words used in Scriptures have to be examined carefully for their usage in not just the local *context* but in other parts of the Bible. In other words, a word like *forever* or *eternity* has to be examined not just in context but in *every* usage in the Bible. And, where possible, compared to usage in the era in which it was written (for example, other first-century writers using the same Greek word), and—bonus points—by the same Bible writer in the same Bible book. Those words have different connotations today than they did back then, so it requires a careful study of all the instances of a particular word.

Hell No

In his book *Recovering the Unity of the Bible*, Walter C. Kaiser Jr. remarks on how astonishing it is that such a work as the Bible could teach a consistent view of God and doctrine since it was written in three languages by some forty authors representing three continents from a diverse background (shepherd, king, prophet, priest, fisherman, etc.) and spanning almost sixteen hundred years. He notes:

> When one adds to this mix the extraordinary variety of literary types ... and the history of the nation of Israel and the early beginnings of the church, it seems incredible to suppose that there could be any kind of unity and coherence ...
>
> Often objections were raised against the older testament even by those who professed to believe in the later testament. How could there be any kind of harmony between the two testaments when there seemed to be serious contradictions and discontinuities present? Heading the list of objections against granting to the Old Testament equal status with the new was the way God was depicted in the Old Testament.[1]

Surely, only a book "breathed on" by God's Holy Spirit could paint a completely consistent picture of God's nature. These types of apparent inconsistencies, Kaiser says, are due to objections that are "unfairly leveled against God in that [those who voice such objections] have little or no appreciation for the full context of the passage or the culture."[2]

The key point to remember through all of this is the foundational premise of Bible study: that the Bible is consistent and will not teach contradictory or varied "truths." Jesus said, "I am the truth" (John 14:6). Not "I am just one of the truths out there." Not "I am the truth that is subject to personal interpretation." There are no "alternate facts."

Let's agree that "truth is truth." Period.

---

1. Kaiser, *Unity*, 85–86.
2. Kaiser, *Unity*, 97.

CHAPTER 1

God's Character—Why It Matters

As we consider an overview of what this book will cover, I want to talk about why any of this matters. I want to talk about God's character. His heart.

One of the most endearing qualities of God is his mercy. And the greatest expression of that mercy is shown in his act of love in sending his Son Jesus to be born as a human and die as a sacrifice to redeem us and save us from the penalty of our inherited sin. In this selfless act, God has made a way for us to be with him for eternity in a perfect world—the world he intended for humans to inhabit since the foundation of that world.

When the Bible says that, in the kingdom to come, "suffering will be no more," that's exactly what it means. "There shall be no more death, nor sorrow, nor crying. There shall be no more pain, for the former things have passed away." (Rev 21:4 NKJV). *Passed away* always means gone, completely eradicated from existence. In the pages to come, you will see that this truth is not conditional, applying to only believers. No one will suffer for eternity—period.

When death and *hades* (the grave) are thrown into the lake of fire, we are told "this means the second death." We learn that death is the opposite of life. It is no life. Nonexistence.

In the only Scripture in which Paul mentions the fate of those who don't accept Jesus, he says they will be destroyed. Yes, Jesus comes in a flaming fire (which doesn't burn him or anyone else) "inflicting vengeance on those who do not know God and on those who do not obey the gospel of our Lord Jesus. These will suffer the punishment of eternal *destruction*, separated from the presence of the Lord and from the glory of his might, when he comes to be glorified by his saints" (2 Thess 1:7-10 NRSV, italics mine).

The word destruction (Greek: *olithros*), used five times in the NT, always means . . . wait for it . . . destruction. Ruin, destroy, death (hang in there—we will go over this completely).

Perhaps the most famous Scripture to all Christians is John 3:16, and you'll note that Jesus says, "God so loved the world that he gave his only begotten Son, so that whosoever believeth in him shall not perish but have everlasting life" (KJV). The word *perish* in the Greek Scriptures is *apollymi*, which always means to destroy, to abolish, to put an end to, to be lost, ruined, or rendered useless. *Nowhere* is this word used in Scripture to mean tortured, tormented, or burned eternally as punishment.

Yet, throughout the centuries, famous theologians have taught that hellfire is a fundamental teaching of the Bible. Kenneth Kantzer, a highly respected evangelical leader, proclaimed, "Those who acknowledge Jesus Christ as Lord cannot escape the clear, unambiguous language with which he warns of the awful truth of eternal punishment."[1]

British philosopher and agnostic Bertrand Russell expressed his distaste of the common belief in hellfire and pointedly makes the case, to me, why this matters:

> There is one serious defect to my mind in Christ's moral character, and that is that He believed in hell. I do not myself feel that any person who is really profoundly humane can believe in everlasting punishment. . . . I really do not think that a person with a proper degree of kindliness in his nature would have put fears and terrors of that sort into the world. ... I must say that I think all this doctrine, that hellfire is a punishment for sin, is a doctrine of cruelty. It is a doctrine that put cruelty into the world and gave the world generations of cruel torture; and the Christ of the Gospels, if you take him as his chroniclers represent him, would certainly have to be considered partly responsible for that.[2]

But Jesus isn't "partly responsible for that" teaching. He never taught it. If anyone is "profoundly humane"—to borrow Russell's words—it's Jesus, the Savior who suffered crucifixion to redeem us from our death sentence.

Think how many people might have drawn near to God and accepted Christ as their savior had they not believed as Russell did! Perhaps Russell

---

1. Thornbury, *Who Will Be Saved*, 98.
2. Russell, *Basic Writings*, 593–94.

God's Character—Why It Matters

wouldn't have remained an agnostic if he had been taught the truth from God's Word.

In the Foreword of the book *Rethinking Hell*, editor John G. Stackhouse Jr. argues that those who believe hellfire is a just punishment for sin reason that since God's love and goodness is "infinite," then "any sin against all those infinities must entail infinite suffering." And that means regardless if you commit a "small" sin or a "big" sin, it's only reasonable that you suffer torment forever.

Stackhouse says,

> Really? Pick your favorite horrible villain, from history or from fiction: No one deserves to suffer any less than does he or she? Isn't there something wrong with any theological "equation" that ends up with Caligula/de Sade/Hitler/Stalin = your friend or relative who decided, for whatever reason, not to accept God's salvation? . . .
>
> Wouldn't it be *reassuring* not to have to try to bend one's mind and, worse, one's heart into a shape that could somehow give glory to God for afflicting people forever, that could somehow call majestic what seems obviously monstrous? . . .
>
> God is offended and offended against by sin, and sin must be dealt with thoroughly on God's behalf as well as on any of ours. . . . There is only so much evil one can work in a human lifetime. Infinity just seems immediately, and wildly, out of proportion to a finite amount of sin, however large and virulent.[3]

Yes, our own God-given sense of justice decries the unfairness of such punishment. That's why Jesus's heart's desire is that all will repent and be saved so they *might not die and be dead forever*. In fact, in 2 Peter 3:9 NIV we read: "[God] is patient with you, not wanting anyone to perish [note it does not say "tortured eternally in fire"] but everyone to come to repentance."

For, those who do not accept Jesus's propitiatory (covering) sacrifice cannot have their sins blotted out. If those sins are not nailed to the cross with Christ, their sin remains. And . . . the wages of sin is death.

Jesus painted several word pictures to portray the utter destruction of the wicked. For example: weeds that are bound in bundles to be burned (Matt 13:30–40), bad fish that is thrown away (Matt 13:48), harmful plants that are rooted up (Matt 15:13), fruitless trees that are cut down (Luke 13:7), and withered branches that are burned (John 15:6). In every parable,

---

3. Date, *Rethinking Hell*, xi–xii.

in every utterance, Jesus points to destruction, whether literally, poetically, or symbolically.

You will learn through these many pages and hundreds of Scriptures in this study that no one anywhere, ever, will be tortured in agonizing pain in some horrific fire for eternity. God's reaction to those who sacrificed their children to gods in burning fire was disgust and outrage. "You shall not worship the Lord your God in that way, for every abominable thing that *the Lord hates* they have done for their gods, for they even burn their sons and their daughters in the fire to their gods" (Deut 12:31 ESV, italics mine).

"They even burn" shows that, of *all* the things the Lord hates, this is most despicable.

The God who does not take the delight in the death of anyone wicked (Ezek 33:11) surely does not take delight in watching anyone suffer—or instigating that torture—and certainly not for eternity.

What you believe on this topic matters. When *The Christian Post* interviewed "hell expert" and Bible scholar Edward Fudge, he was asked: "Is it important for the average Christian to know what happens in hell, or is this more for theologians?" he answered:

> It matters . . . because this has to do very much with the character of God, and the way people view God's character. . . . Are we supposed to think that the God who loves the world so much that he gave his only son so believers would not perish but have eternal life is going to then turn around and throw billions of them into something resembling a lake of volcanic lava and make it so that cannot die, so they will have to endure this forever[?] That doesn't sound like the God that I know and see in Jesus Christ.
>
> So I believe the traditional view is a horrible scandal against the character of God himself.[4]

What Would Be the Point?

Before you voice objections (I'm hoping all your objections will be satisfyingly resolved when you dig into the Scriptures), think of the conscience and sense of justice God planted in your own heart. What purpose would it serve to punish someone forever by making them endure endless agony? Let's take a logical look at this.

Rationalization #1: The threat of hellfire is a deterrent to sin.

4. Vu, "Interview," paras. 27–30.

God's Character—Why It Matters

Seriously? How has that been effective for the last two thousand years? The world is full of evil and sin, and no amount of hellfire threat has swung the needle toward righteousness. Think about the Crusades, for example. Scaring people into serving God may have produced some converts, but their motivation for being faithful to God is out of fear (terror, not respect, which is the "healthy" fear of the Lord we all should embrace). God wants his children to love him, not be obedient because of terror of punishment. All you have to do is think of a cruel father who beats his child senseless for any infraction of his rules and magnify that cruelty and punishment to the nth degree.

Since "perfect love throws fear outside," there is no way anyone could actually love God in obedience if he is in fear of God. He commands we love him with our whole heart. Just as a child could never love a father who brutalized him over any sin. We know the basic fact: threatening to punish someone, whether with jail or torture, does not deter a person determined to sin.

Let's take this a step further.

This wouldn't be done to serve as a warning to others, to scare them into repenting, for no one in the future will need to or be given the chance to repent. This wouldn't be done to encourage the sufferer to repent, for repentance would not be the objective of the torture or be offered. Eternal torment does not come with a reprieve option.

Rationalization #2: God's sense of justice must be met, and that can only be done by tormenting "souls" in a hellfire for eternity.

What feeling of satisfaction or "sense of justice" would God, the angels, or anyone on earth experience by watching humans suffer in such a manner? How could Jesus claim "suffering will be no more" if suffering continues forever? How could you love God and enjoy "the pleasures of his presence forever" (Ps 16:11) if you knew that somewhere, either within your purview or not, those you once loved—perhaps your children, your spouse, your siblings, your parents, or your best friend—were screaming in excruciating pain every second into eternity, all to supposedly satisfy God's sense of justice?

The words used to mollify those who find this prospect unpleasant (to put it mildly) are that God's ways and thoughts are not ours, and we just have to accept this is what a just and righteous God will and must do. I hope that consolation is as weak and unsatisfying to you as it is to me.

I posit that so long as followers of Jesus believe that this is what their loving, merciful, kind, and fair God is like, they can never truly love, trust, and worship him fully. Could you truly love your earthly father if you knew he secretly tortured people in his basement (regardless of whether he claimed to enjoy it or did it because he felt he must)?

Our sense of right and wrong, of justice and mercy, comes from God, and, as flawed beings, surely we cannot be more just than God. Yet, we would never, ever think of such a punishment for even the most wicked of the wicked. Truly, the equitable, merciful, and appropriate punishment for those who refuse Jesus's sacrifice is for them to die (not be tortured for eternity) in their sins, which is, in fact, what Jesus warned would happen to the religious leaders of his day (John 8:21). Of all the people Jesus vocally and pointedly condemned when he walked the earth, it was those religious leaders. Surely if hellfire torment was on the menu, Jesus would have told them at that moment. But, no—instead he said they would die in their sins. That was to be their punishment.

If you believe that eternal torment is what the wicked deserve for their sin, the notion is contrary to Scripture, which says "the wages [penalty, price, cost] of sin is death (Rom 6:33). *Death* is sin's payment. And because Jesus came and gave his perfect life as a propitiation (covering) sacrifice to cancel out the sin we inherit from Adam, the price for our sin is paid *when we die*. That's why Hebrews 2:9 says Christ tasted death for all people. Since he tasted it, we don't have to swallow the penalty.

John Stott, the famous Anglican priest and theologian who is credited with starting the evangelical movement, wrote this:

> Emotionally, I find the concept [of eternal torment] intolerable and do not understand how people can live with it without either cauterizing their feelings or cracking under the strain. But our emotions are a fluctuating, unreliable guide to truth and must not be exalted to the place of supreme authority in determining it. As a committed Evangelical, my question must be and is not what my heart tells me, but what does God's word say? And in order to answer this question, we need to survey the biblical material afresh and to open our minds (not just our hearts) to the possibility that Scripture points in the direction of annihilationism, and that "eternal conscious torment" is a tradition which has to yield to the supreme authority of Scripture.[5]

---

5. Edwards, *Essentials*, 314.

Yield to the supreme authority of Scripture. Yep, that's the ticket.

This is what every true follower of Christ should yearn to do in all things.

Let me repeat this: the price for our sin is death. That is the only wage we pay. Nowhere will you find a verse that says something like "the wages of sin is eternal torment." And, in addition, does eternal (forever—billions and billions of years and on and on) torture seem like the just and balanced payment for sinning for a mere *few* years of human life? Wouldn't it make more sense that *if* one were to be tortured, the amount of time should equal the time spent sinning? Just saying . . .

We will see in passage after passage that God clearly lays out specific punishments for those who disobey him, and they never include torment in fire for eternity—or any torment other than a temporary emotional one (weeping and gnashing of teeth—discussed later). And it is appointed for a person to die only once (Heb 9:27). And, yes, the writer of Hebrews does say after that is "judgment." But judgment, like death and hell, are not what you think or what you've been taught. Bear with me, and let's take this slowly.

To Dust You Return

Adam sinned, and God returned him to the dust from which he came. He wasn't sent to some nebulous realm to be tortured forever. God said plainly: "From dust [Hebrew: *dakka*] you are and from dust you will return" (Gen 3:19). Moses, the man given commandments directly by God, said, "You turn people back to dust, saying, 'Return to dust, you mortals'" (Ps 90:3 NIV). Nothing about some heading off to suffer eternal torment. Every person, everyone, goes back to dust.

When we understand from the Scriptures that death is the end or absence of life, and the soul (Hebrew: *nephesh*) that sins will die (Ezek 18:4), confusion and contradictions dissipate.

Ponder this last thought before we dig deep into Scripture. If the punishment for sin is eternal torment in a hellfire, then Jesus would have to endure that punishment to be an equal (life for a life) sacrifice for our sins and garner forgiveness for us. For us to be declared righteous and be saved, Jesus would now and forever have to suffer agony in hellfire. Don't miss this point.

There is only one sacrifice for sin: Jesus's death on the cross, which the Bible says is perfect and sufficient. No other sacrifice is needed. He paid the price once, for all time. That is because the wages of sin is death, not eternal torment (Heb 10:11–14). He gave his perfect human life in exchange for Adam's. He died (Rev 1:18).

All the Bible writers understood that because of Adam's disobedience, their future would entail returning to the dust of the ground. The hope of resurrection, given in divine inspiration to Isaiah, was that one day "your dead will live, Lord; their bodies will rise—let those who dwell in the dust wake up and shout for joy—your dew is like the dew of the morning; the earth will give birth to her dead" (Isa 26:19 NIV). Did you catch that bit about who wakes up and where they're residing? He says the dead are dwelling in the dust, and their bodies will rise.

Jesus three times in the book of John pointedly stated: "For my Father's will is that everyone who looks to the Son and believes in him shall have eternal life, and I will raise them up at the last day" (John 6:40 NIV).

Jesus also said in John 5:28 (NLT): "Indeed, the time is coming when all the dead in their graves will hear the voice of God's Son, and they will rise again. Those who have done good will rise to experience eternal life, and those who have continued in evil will rise to experience judgment."

He didn't say some of the dead would rise. He didn't say only the wicked would come out of their graves because the righteous are already with him in heaven. He said *everyone* in history who has died will come out of their graves (Rev 20:13 says also "the sea gave up those dead in it") and be judged.

Everyone—the good and the evil—will one day, in the last "day," be resurrected from the dead—not before. A specific day or period of time that is *yet future* (because, simply, we have not seen all the billions of people who have died from Adam on down raised back to life).

We know, at very least, this judgment period is not just one of a judge declaring a sentence. Multiple times in the gospels, Jesus speaks about how the people of Sodom and Gomorrah *will fare better* in the judgment ("it will be more bearable," "they will be better off," "it will be more tolerable"— please note the future tense Jesus uses: "it will be") than some of those in Jesus's day, because if those sinners had seen his miracles, they would have repented (Matt 10:15; 11:24). Paul says in Acts 24:15 that "there will be a resurrection of both the righteous and the unrighteous."

If Christians, as some are taught, are raptured into heaven in spirit bodies, how can they then hear Jesus's voice and come out from the grave? They can't. How would you justify that ubiquitous church teaching?

One pastor I asked said that believers will be raptured to heaven temporarily as spirits. Then, at some future point, God would put them back on earth (I suppose in a dead body rotting under the ground?), then would resurrect that believer from the dead body back into a spirit body.

Would you please join with me in saying, "Huh?"

Since Jesus promises the meek will inherit the earth, and that he will reign on the earth for a thousand years, what would the spirits of the saints be doing in heaven, living in the spirit realm? (Rev 20:6; cf. 1 Cor 15:20–26).

Once you understand what the Scriptures teach about the definition of the words *spirit* and *soul*, you will soon begin to understand that the Bible is true and consistent when it says that "The heavens belong to the LORD, but he has given the earth to all humanity." (Ps 115:16 NLT). God's glorious kingdom as depicted in Revelation 21 comes down from heaven *to earth* so that God will reside with mankind the way he did with Adam, fulfilling his original purpose (Rev 21:2–3).

God's Word Always Brings the Results He Intends

God says the word that goes forth from his mouth does not return without the results he intended (Isa 55:11). What did he intend for humans? He intended for humans to live in fellowship here *on earth* with God. The ending of the Bible shows that his original plan will never be thwarted; it comes to fulfillment with humanity living forever on earth, a renewed and blessed earth relieved of the curse (Rev 22:3). Where will the curse be lifted? Here, from the earth, our planet, where we live. Why lift the curse if blessed and redeemed humanity flies off to heaven? Or is relocated to some new planet somewhere else in the galaxy?

This is so important to delve into because it is in harmony with the Bible's teachings on the spirit and soul. Why put your hope in a heavenly home when it is not what God promises or intends for his human creation? I hear all kinds of convoluted explanations, from laypeople and theologians, of how Christians will live in heaven though there is no doubt that humans will inhabit the new earth for eternity.

Remember: all Scripture is inspired of God and useful in correction and reproving, for setting things straight. The few Scriptures that seem to contradict these truths will be explored further in this study, and you will see that the context and the meanings of the words will reveal doctrine that is in perfect harmony with the rest of the Bible. For it must.

Peter warned in 2 Peter 3:16 (NIV), speaking of the apostle Paul: "His letters contain some things that are hard to understand, which ignorant and unstable people distort, as they do the other Scriptures, to their own destruction" (note: he said *destruction* not *eternal torment*). Even back then, when some of the apostles were still alive and could teach firsthand doctrine given to them from Jesus himself, people struggled with the deep truths of God. So it's no wonder that we wrestle with doctrine. And—let me be clear—I am in no way saying that anyone who believes differently about a doctrine or two than I do is going to face God's wrath—God's wrath is coming against "those who do not know God and do not obey the gospel of our Lord Jesus" (2 Thess 1:8 NIV). Not because one person believes one thing about the resurrection and his fellow believer interprets Scripture another way.

Who knows why God made it so challenging to get to the heart of the truth about so many things in his Word? I'll be the first to admit that some things in the Bible are hard to understand. But God's Word is a light to our roadway, and those who ask God in faith for wisdom will be given it (James 1:5). However, wisdom often comes at a cost.

Many pastors and theologians who have come to see the overwhelming evidence in the Bible for "annihilism" over eternal torment have, throughout the centuries, been attacked, persecuted, and even killed. Pastor Gregory Stump shares in the Preface to *Rethinking Hell* that over the years "I have often faced alienation and marginalization from peers who have vehemently disagreed with me, along with the ongoing potential of losing my job over the view of hell that I held." He adds:

> Traditionalists are adamant that there are no credible reasons for holding our view. At times, the experience of being dismissed by others as emotional, eccentric, or even heretical, combined with others' unwillingness to actually review the evidence for conditionalism [conditional immortality] has been both confusing and deeply troubling, particularly given the fact that evangelicals claim to base their beliefs on their study of Scripture.[6]

We are all responsible to God for our faith and the way we worship him. Jesus said God is looking for those who will worship him in "spirit and in truth" (John 4:24). Prayerfully consider everything you study, and before you jump to any conclusions based on a handful of verses that appear to be teaching something contrary to the entire body of Scripture, remember

---

6. Date, *Rethinking Hell*, xv, xvii.

God's Character—Why It Matters

that the Word of God is wholly consistent, and if 98 percent of Scripture teaches one consistent doctrine or understanding of a topic, the 2 percent that seems to be teaching the opposite must be explained in a way that is scripturally in harmony with that 98 percent. It cannot be any other way.

That's the key, right there. Try to have fun digging for wisdom. It's more precious than gold or silver, and the truth will set you free indeed (John 8:32). Regardless of what every church in the world might teach.

Go to the source. God promises to give *you* wisdom if you ask for it. He doesn't say he'll answer that prayer by giving it to your pastor or priest or reverend for you. And always remember—God's character matters.

PART 1:
DEATH AND RESURRECTION

CHAPTER 2

The Soul and Death

BEFORE YOU CAN UNDERSTAND what the future holds for all humans in the resurrection, you have to start at the basics, and that is with terminology. We continually hear diverse and contradictory definitions for the words that are translated as soul, spirit, death, and hell. Just today as I was writing this, I listened to a sermon in which the person preaching kept emphasizing how we have a soul within us, something separate from our physical body. Spirit was defined as our true nature, yet this sermon left a patina of confusion when she stated that we worship God in spirit, in some spiritual way or body, even though, supposedly, the soul is the "thing" we are inside us.

Here's an explanation of the second coming of Christ presented by the Moody Bible Institute, and it's pretty typical of what the evangelical body around the world believes and teaches and which you will soon learn is completely in opposition to Scripture (you will see what we're up against when we question "authority"):

> Before He establishes His kingdom on earth, Jesus will come for His Church, an event commonly referred to as the "Rapture." At that time the dead in Christ will be raised and living Christians will be caught up to meet the Lord in the air and be with him forever. In this resurrection, those who have died in Christ will have their redeemed souls and spirits united with a body similar to Christ's glorified body. Christians living at the time of this event will not die, but will be changed to be like Christ. . . . At the end of the Tribulation, Jesus Christ will return with the hosts of heaven as well as the Church to establish the Messianic Kingdom on earth.[1]

1. Moody Bible Institute, "The Second Coming," 3–7, 15.

I hope that by the time you finish studying God's Word—not my word—in this exploration of Bible truth, you will come to understand that *everything* in that statement is unscriptural (did you catch the bit about redeemed souls *and* spirits? Implying there are two different forms, components, or entities that go to heaven?). Yes, that may sound like a lot of hubris on my part—from someone without any formal training or advanced degree in Bible studies or theology. But don't take my word for any of this material. Study all the Scriptures provided. Do your own digging. And do it prayerfully, because—remember—God gives wisdom to those who humbly seek it and without reproach.

That said, the single most important question one can ask is "What happens to me when I die?" Are we dead forever? Do we wander in some ethereal world of limbo? Or, as most churches teach, do we have a soul that goes to heaven when we die if we are good or gets sent to a burning hell or lake of fire if we're judged to be evil?

Genesis 2:7 (ESV) says: "Then the LORD God formed the man of dust from the ground and breathed into his nostrils the breath of life, and the man became a living creature."

Many other translations say the man became "a living soul." The Hebrew word here is *nephesh*. Biblical usage includes definitions of a breathing creature, soul, self, life, creature, person, appetite, mind, living being, desire, emotion, passion.

Note that man *became* a living soul, not that he was *given* a soul. This is a far cry from the universal belief that man is in possession of an immortal soul. In fact, the expression "immortal soul" does not occur in the Scriptures even once.

Let me repeat that. Neither the words, term, concept, or teaching ever occurs in the Bible even once.

God told Adam that in the day he should eat of the forbidden tree he would surely die (Gen 2:17). And if Adam could die, then he was not immortal. It wasn't until Greek philosophy and Gnostic mystical teachings seeped into the early church that Christians were introduced to this concept.

Some argue in error that when Adam did die, he died a "spiritual death," for, they say, he was a spiritual being. But Paul tells us,

> Thus it is written, "The first man Adam became a living being"; the last Adam became a life-giving spirit. But it is not the spiritual that is first but the natural, and then the spiritual. The first man was

from the earth, a man of dust; the second man is from heaven. As was the man of dust, so also are those who are of the dust, and as is the man of heaven, so also are those who are of heaven. (1 Cor 15:45–47 ESV)

Adam was not "a spiritual being having an earthly experience," as I've heard some believers describe our collective human experience, but a living soul made from the literal dust, even as God had said plainly, "For you are dust, and to dust you shall return" (Gen 3:19 ESV).

Adam's punishment was death, the end of his being a soul or living creature. Dust is not alive, conscious, or suffering torment anywhere. God sent Adam back to where he came from—"to dust you will return"—a place of nonexistence, which is what the Bible consistently teaches is the condition of the dead (see Job 10:9; Dan 12:2; Ps 103:14). The Bible simply says that God made man out of the dust (elements of soil) of the ground. Adam was 100 percent material, organic. We don't see God take some ethereal spirit essence and put it inside Adam.

In fact, it was Satan, the serpent in the garden, who implied that death did not really mean nonexistence. Satan told Eve, "You will not surely die. For God knows that when you eat of [the forbidden fruit] your eyes will be opened, and you will be like God, knowing good and evil" (Gen 3:4).

Not surprising, this lie about being immortal ("you will not die") comes from the father of the lie. Don't believe the lie.

Souls Die—Plain and Simple

"The soul who sins shall die" (Ezek 18:4). It's a simple equation that is reiterated throughout Scripture, in both the OT and NT. The wages of sin is death, so any soul that sins has to pay the price: death.

This truth was pounded home in the OT through the system of sacrifices. The penalty or payment for the worst commission of sin was death, whether animal or human. Torture was never part of the equation.

James Dunn, British New Testament scholar, says, "The manner in which the sin offering dealt with sin was by its death. The sacrificial animal, identified with the offerer in his sin, had to be destroyed in order to destroy the sin which it embodied. The sprinkling, smearing and pouring away of the sacrificial blood in the sight of God indicated that the life was wholly destroyed, and with it the sin and the sinner."[2]

The sin, therefore, is destroyed along with the body.

A soul can die because we *are* souls; we don't *possess* souls. Animals are souls, and if we look in Genesis chapter 1, we see that *nephesh* is used to describe fish in the sea and animals on the earth. Note, too, that in Numbers 19:1, *nephesh* is used for a dead body. A dead body is a dead soul.

Interestingly, Paul says there is only one "who alone has immortality," and that is Christ Jesus (1 Tim 6:16). He alone. That means no one before Jesus at the time of Paul's writing had immortality (cf. 1 Cor 15:18, which says Christians are still "asleep," and we'll look at this expression in a later chapter). Jesus was the first to be resurrected to immortal life (1 Cor 15:20), and when Christ returns, those who "belong to Christ" will be *made* alive (verse 23). Which makes perfect sense. Death was "passed on to all men, for all have sinned" (Rom 5:12)—that is, with the exception of Jesus, who alone was sinless (Heb 4:15).

Humans Do Not Have Inherent Immortality

It's so important to understand that humans do not have inherent immortality. This was a pervasive Greek teaching that filtered into the church after Jesus died. Humans are *gifted* with immortality in Jesus's kingdom via the resurrection through their faith in Jesus's atoning sacrifice.

Humans who are welcomed into the kingdom in the future will be granted immortality, for then, and only then, will death be swallowed up forever. When there is no more death, then humans will have endless life. Not because they will be given "an immortal soul" or that they already have "an immortal soul inside them."

Think. Where would Adam and Eve be right now if they hadn't sinned? They would be here, on earth, *as* souls, living forever in perfect organic human bodies. To prevent the first humans from living forever on the earth—and their offspring—God barred the entrance to the garden of Eden and hence prevented access to the tree of life (Gen 3:22–23). He even posted some angels with a flaming, spinning sword at that spot just to ensure they would get the point (verse 24).

If Adam and Eve were alive today, they would have what Jesus promises every faithful believer: "But the water that I shall give him will

2. Bacchiocchi, *Immortality or Resurrection*, 227.

become in him a fountain of water springing up into everlasting life." (John 4:13-14 NKJV). Adam and Eve would have never returned to the dust of the ground. They would have had perpetual renewing life force pumping through their bodies for eternity. And if we are faithful and believe in the Son of God, we too will live endlessly without dying after being raised to life in the resurrection.

Paul wrote: "Behold I shew you a mystery; We shall not all sleep, but we shall all be changed" (1 Cor 15:51 KJV). This change comes at the resurrection, according to 1 Corinthians 15:53: "For this corruptible must put on incorruption, and this mortal must put on immortality." Compare this with Romans 2:7, which says that God will render to each one according to his deeds: "to those who by patience in well-doing seek for glory and honor and immortality, he will *give* eternal life" (ESV, italics mine).

Did you catch that? A person isn't inherently immortal. Humans are mortal with corruptible (Greek: *phthartos*: perishing, destructible) bodies. It's only through faith and obedience to Christ that one gets to "put on incorruption" (unperishable, indestructible). We are encouraged by Paul to "seek immortality." We wouldn't need to seek it if we already have it. Make sense?

This is the only escape from death—there is no other way but by and through our savior Jesus Christ, who has "abolished death, and hath brought life and immortality to light through the gospel" (2 Tim 1:10 KJV).

The Use of "Soul" in the New Testament

The only word used in the New Testament for soul is *psuche* (also spelled *psyche*). It's found 105 times, but it's translated *soul* only 58 times. In other instances you'll see this word translated as *life, mind, heart, us,* and *you*. It's important to be aware of these other uses.

As we see in the OT, psuche is used for both humans and animals. Revelation 16:3 (KJV) says: "And the second angel poured out his vial upon the sea; and it became as the blood of a dead man: and every living soul died in the sea." This is consistent with the usage we see in Genesis through Malachi—that living creatures are souls; they do not contain souls. And souls die. There are many verses in the NT that show the word used for people or an individual (see Acts 2:41-43; 7:14; Rom 2:9; 13:1; Jas 5:20; 1 Pet 3:20 for a few examples). In Matthew 16:26, Jesus uses psuche to mean life (eternal life prospects) when he says, "For what is a man profited, if he shall gain the whole world, and lose his own soul? or what shall a man give in exchange for his soul?" (KJV).

Jesus urges people to follow him because they will find rest for their *souls* due to his light yoke (Matt 11:29). Even God mentions how his own soul is well pleased by Jesus (Matt 12:18), which we can assume is God's person or being. Surely God himself does not have some kind of nebulous "spirit body" within him. Mark 10:45 KJV tells us, "For even the Son of man came not to be ministered unto but to minister, and to give his life [soul—*psuche*] a ransom for many." Jesus certainly wasn't talking about some invisible entity within him either. He gave his mortal, human life—the perfect equivalent for Adam—to ransom or buy back the human race, who had all sinned because of descending from Adam (Rom 5:12–21). A soul for a soul.

Nowhere will you find in the NT the use of psuche for an immortal soul, and that's what we would expect since the Bible must be consistent from start to finish.

CHAPTER 3

What Is the Spirit?

IF HUMANS ARE SOULS, then what is the spirit?

It is the breath that animates and gives our flesh or body life or soul, and without this breath or spirit, we die. "For the body without the spirit is dead" (Jas 2:26).

All living souls have the "breath of life." This is the mysterious energizing force that animates all souls and that dissipates as it seeps out of the body at death.

The website The Four Questions of Judaism makes this astute observation:

> What is the connection of breath to soul? It turns out that in the biblical mind-set such a connection was not only possible, it was almost obvious. What was it that invigorated the body to give it life? Was it the blood? That was impossible since blood was present in a corpse. Any other fluid or any organ would have the same problem. It was only the breath that appeared to be present in living things and not present after death. Looked upon this way, it was obvious that life came from the breath.[1]

The Spirit Returns to God

In Ecclesiastes chapter 12, Solomon paints a picture of what happens to people when they get old, and, finally, after the body has broken down fully. He says, "Then the dust will return to the earth as it was, And the spirit will

---

1. Four Questions of Judaism, 'Neshama—Breath or Soul," lines 38–45.

return to God who gave it" (verse 7 NKJV). The Hebrew word for spirit is *ruach* (not nephesh, which is *soul*).

We noted earlier that Adam and all animals, fish, and birds are souls. God breathed into Adam "the breath of life" in order for him to become a living soul (Gen 2:7). The Hebrew word used for "breath of life" is *neshamah*.

In Luke 23:46, Jesus cried out to God just before he died: "Father, into Thy hands I commend My spirit" (KJV).

Another word or expression we see in the OT is "breathed his last" (Hebrew: *gava*). In some translations like the King James Bible the expression "gave up the ghost" is used. In Genesis 25:8 we see how Abraham breathed his last and died in a good old age (see Gen 35:29 and 49:29, where this expression is used upon Isaac's and Jacob's deaths respectively).

Some try to argue that what God breathed into Adam was an invisible immortal soul that would continue to exist after his body returned to dust. But there is nothing in Scripture to support such a claim. In Job 33:4 we read: "The spirit [ruach] of God has made me, and the breath [neshamah] of the Almighty gives me life" (NKJV). This parallelism implies the two terms are interchangeable. (We see another parallelism with these two words at Job 27:3.)

Of course, spirit is more than breath, because if someone dies and you pump air into his lungs, that by itself won't reanimate the body. Sometimes people stop breathing and seem dead, yet you can resuscitate them. That implies the spirit that gives them life is still present. Once that spirit is gone, all the oxygen in the world will do no good. Interestingly, God told Noah: "But you shall not eat flesh with its life, that is, its blood" (Gen 9:4 ESV). We modern folks know that blood is responsible for carrying oxygen to every cell in the body. It stands to reason there is some important biological and spiritual connection between the spirit and the life force in blood.

In Ezekiel chapter 37, we're given a vision of a valley of dry bones. The prophet Ezekiel is instructed to "prophesy to the breath [ruach] … say to the breath, 'Thus says the Lord God: "Come from the four winds, O breath, and breathe on these slain, that they may live"'" (verse 9 NKJV). Ezekiel does as God commands, and the inanimate skeletons come alive and stand on their feet (verse 10). The word used throughout this passage that is translated as breath (sometimes wind or winds) is the Hebrew word for spirit. It takes more than air to animate these bones; they need the breath of life—the spirit.

What Is the Spirit?

Now, just because you have the breath of life, that doesn't mean you have *eternal* life. Since life is a gift from God, and eternal life is *conditional* upon acceptance of Jesus's sacrifice to cover sin so we could be declared righteous (2 Cor 5:21), the spirit or breath of life is in God's hands. Jesus knew that when he commended his spirit into God's hands. He was depending on God to raise him from the dead, and that necessitated God to reanimate his dead body into a glorified resurrected body with spirit. Hebrews 5:7 (NLT) says, "While Jesus was here on earth, he offered prayers and pleadings, with a loud cry and tears, to the one who could rescue him from death."

This is further made clear in Ecclesiastes 12:7: "The dust returns to the earth as it was, and the spirit returns to God who gave it" (ESV). The spirit doesn't go flying back through the sky to heaven. Just as when someone dies and their land deed reverts back to the bank, the ownership of the spirit of a creature—its future fate—is back in God's court to do with what he will.

Biblical Parallelism

Let me explain a bit about this writing style called parallelism in the Bible that can be very helpful in understanding some terms. We see this in the Psalms a lot, where something is stated one way, then reiterated another way—but meaning the same thing.

Job 34:14–15 states: "If [God] should take back his spirit to himself, and gather to himself his breath, all flesh would perish together, and man would return to the dust" (KJV). The parallelism shows that God's breath equates to his life-giving Spirit.

So long as creatures have this "breath of life," they are "living souls." But when the breath leaves, they become dead souls. When Jesus raised Jairus's daughter back to life, it says "her spirit came again" (Luke 8:55 KJV). An immortal, disembodied spirit didn't fly back into her body. Rather, as what is described of an Egyptian in 1 Samuel 30:11–12, her body was reanimated, flushed again with life force. When David was pursuing the raiding Amalekites, "they found an Egyptian in the field, and brought him to David, and gave him bread, and he did eat; and they made him drink water; and they gave him a piece of a cake of figs, and two clusters of raisins: and when he had eaten, his spirit [ruach] came again to him" (KJV). This Egyptian wasn't dead; he merely needed some reviving, reanimation. We need to be aware of the various nuances of this word *spirit*—but understand it is never used in Scripture to mean some entity or ethereal body residing inside humans.

It is God's life-giving Spirit that gives life, Jesus says in John 6:63. Without it, we are just "flesh," and "the flesh profits nothing." He goes on to say, "The words that I speak to you are spirit and they are life" (NKJV). His words are spirit or breath to those who accept him because Jesus is the way, the truth, and the life (John 14:6), and embracing his words is what will lead to a fountain of everlasting life or spirit/breath bubbling up from within our soon-to-be immortal bodies.

CHAPTER 4

The State of the Dead in the Old Testament

Senseless people do not know, fools do not understand,
that though the wicked spring up like grass and all evildoers flourish,
they will be destroyed forever.

—Psalm 92:6–7 NIV

DO THE DEAD SLEEP in an unconscious state until the resurrection? Or does something survive death and go to heaven, where God dwells—or to some hellfire, where a person in some indestructible form suffers torment? People have asked these questions for hundreds of years.

To reiterate: both the Old Testament and the New Testament must be consistent. Because there are only a handful of passages in the Bible that appear to be at odds with the whole of scriptural teaching, we are going to look at every one of them. We have to. Otherwise someone, at some point, will use one lone passage to "prove" some doctrine like the immortality of the soul, or that Enoch was the first to go to heaven because "God took him" (Gen 5:24), or that bad people will burn forever in the lake of fire because in Revelation it says they'll be thrown into it (Rev 20:15).

Thankfully, the Bible is such a rich book with Scripture after Scripture that form a solid teaching on nearly every topic. And, thankfully, the Bible, being "God-breathed," is reliable. We can bet our lives on its truth, and we should.

So, let's start first in the Old Testament and work our way through on this important subject of the state of the dead. Now that you understand that souls are living things and the spirit is a living being's life force, let's look at hell or the grave.

Sheol—Where You Go When You Die

To understand the Hebrew Scriptures' teaching on death, you merely have to look at one word: *sheol*. This word is commonly used in the Old Testament to speak of the resting place of the dead. Out of the sixty-five times it is used, *never* is it suggested that sheol is a place of punishment for the ungodly (hell) or a place of conscious existence for anyone or any animal that is dead. Did I say "never"?

Different translations of the Bible translate sheol in different ways. For example: in the King James Version of the Bible, sheol is translated thirty-one times as the grave, thirty-one times as hell, and three times as the pit. These inconsistencies in translation give way to misinterpretation, especially when verses are taken out of context and the whole Bible isn't considered. That's why it is so important for any student of the Bible to dig into the actual words and their meanings at the time of writing and compare to *all other usages in the Bible*. It can be easily done with so many online sites like Blue Letter Bible, which has features showing not only the Hebrew and Greek words used but their many meanings and all Scriptures using those words. And you can use Strong's concordance to see every Greek word used in the Bible, each word's meanings, and every instance of its use.

For instance, if you pull up Psalm 16:10 from the King James Bible, you get: "For thou wilt not leave my soul in hell." Someone taking that verse by itself might think it means "God won't leave my soul tormented in hellfire" (which would contradict their typical understanding of hellfire being a place of *eternal* torment from which there is no reprieve). Such a reading is an obvious misinterpretation of the text, clarified if reading the Revised Standard Version: "For thou does not give me up to Sheol," that is, the grave. The psalmist here expresses confidence that God would not abandon him in the grave, and this is confirmed in the New Testament when that *exact* verse is applied in Acts 2:27 to Christ, who was not left in the grave (Greek: *hades*) by his Father.

In Job 14:13, Job asks God to hide him in sheol (the grave) until God's wrath passed and appoint a time to remember him and bring him back to life. Surely if Job believed hell was a place of torment, he wouldn't have asked to be hidden there. His life was the cruelest of torment when he

The State of the Dead in the Old Testament

prayed this. It's clear he believed being in "hell" (sheol, the grave or pit of the dead, the unconscious state of nothingness) would be a welcome relief. And in chapter 3 he moans: "Why did I not die at birth, come forth from the womb and expire? . . . For then I should have lain down and been quiet; I should have slept; then I should have been at rest. . . . There the wicked cease from troubling and there the weary are at rest" (verses 11, 13, 17). Not just the wicked but the righteous, too, rest in death. Isaiah 57:2 assures us: "Those who walk uprightly enter into peace; they find rest as they lie in death" (NIV).

Young or old, righteous or wicked, those going to sheol find a place of "rest." While the word *nuwach* used here for *rest* has a myriad of meanings in the Bible, literal and figurative, it's clear that when used in conjunction with sheol it means to cease, to be relieved of all human cares.

Remember: the Bible must be and is consistent. If any verses appear to be teaching something wholly in opposition to the rest of Scripture and the understood meaning of a word in biblical times and usage, the interpretation is incorrect.

It's helpful to keep in mind that different translations often reflect the theological convictions of the translators. For example, the translators of the KJV believed that at death the righteous go to heaven and the wicked to hell. Consequently, they translated sheol "grave" when referring to the righteous, whose bodies rested in the grave, and "hell" when referring to the wicked, whose souls are supposedly tormented in a place of punishment. This inconsistency can trip you up if you aren't careful.

John W. Cooper, professor of philosophical theology at Calvin Theological Seminary, writes this in his book *Body, Soul, and Life Everlasting*:

> Perhaps most interesting for traditional Christians to note is the fact that [sheol] is the resting place of the dead irrespective of their religion during life. Sheol is not the "hell" to which the wicked are condemned and from which the Lord's faithful are spared in glory. . . . There is no doubt that believers and unbelievers all were thought to go to sheol when they die.[1]

The Interpreter's Dictionary of the Bible concurs: "Nowhere in the Old Testament is the abode of the dead regarded as a place of punishment or torment. The concept of an infernal 'hell' developed in Israel only during the Hellenistic period."[2]

1. Cooper, *Body, Soul, and Life Everlasting*, 55.
2. Fudge, *The Fire That Consumes*, 44.

Sheol is described as a deep place, a place where those who die "go down" to, which makes sense as a euphemism for being buried under the ground.

Let me interject something important. The Bible is a collection of literal, figurative, and poetic passages. Sometimes it's obvious a Bible writer is speaking in allegory or poetic imagery (such as describing the trees clapping their hands—Isa 55:12), but other times it may not be so obvious. That's when those three C's (consistency, character, and context) must be brought into play. Don't take everything literally! God expects you to use the brain he gave you to reason logically.

Sheol is contrasted with the high heavens, for in death we are as far away (deep) from God as possible. Amos 9:2 (ESV) says: "If they dig into Sheol, from there shall my hand take them; if they climb up to heaven, from there I will bring them down" (clearly a figurative passage). Psalm 139:7-8 KJV says, "Where shall I go from your Spirit? Or where shall I flee from your presence? If I ascend to heaven, you are there! If I make my bed in Sheol, you are there!"

When Jacob mourned Joseph, he said he would "go down to Sheol to my son, mourning" (Gen 37:35 ESV). And when Korah and his rabble defied Moses, the ground rent opened and swallowed them up, "so they and all that belonged to them went down alive to Sheol: and the earth closed over them" (Num 16:31-33 ESV). Surely Moses did not mean their immortal souls somehow stayed alive once the ground closed up, and they went to some realm of torment. No, these souls suffocated as they were buried under mounds of dirt.

Here are some biblical parallelisms that help drive home this understanding.

In the Old Testament, we see the Hebrew word for *pit* (*bowr*) exchanged for sheol at times. For instance, David writes in Psalm 88:3-4 (NIV), "I am set apart with the dead, like the slain who lie in the grave, whom you remember no more, who are cut off from your care. I am counted among those who go down to the pit; I am like one without strength."

The Hebrew word for destruction—*abaddon*—also is used in parallelism with sheol. Job 26:6 (KJV) states, "Hell [sheol] is naked before him, and destruction [abaddon] hath no covering" (see also Proverbs 15:11 and 27:20). Another example of parallelism is found in Psalm 88:10-11: "Do you show your wonders to the dead? Do their spirits rise up and praise you?

The State of the Dead in the Old Testament

Is your love declared in the grave, your faithfulness in Destruction?" (NIV). Sheol, the grave, is the same as destruction. Nothing more, nothing less.

Job calls sheol a "land of deep darkness" (Job 10:21). Psalm 94:17 (NIV) says, "Unless the LORD had given me help, I would soon have dwelt in the silence of death" (cf. Ps 115:17).

King Solomon (in his God-granted wisdom) described sheol as the fate and final resting place of both humans and animals (Eccl 9:2), and where "there is no work or thought or wisdom" (verse 10). If there is no thought, then there can be no conscious suffering. Simply put, "the living know that they will die, but the dead know nothing. . . . Their love and their hate and their envy have already perished" (verses 5–6 ESV).

Some like to claim that Solomon just didn't know about Jesus and the "secret" truth about hellfire and heavenly reward. Seriously?

Remember: truth in the Bible never changes. What is true in Scripture in the OT is true in the NT. And, come to think of it, why would a loving God hide some horrific secret about punishing the wicked in eternal torment? Wouldn't he make it clear from Adam on down that such punishment would await the unfaithful?

The common phrase in the Old Testament "and he slept with his fathers" implies an understanding that those who die join their forebears in the same condition (see 1 Kgs 1:21; 11:43—also check out the chapter "Sleeping in Death").

Job expresses the hope we all should have for the future—not a time when we will be taken to heaven but resurrected here on earth, in perfect flesh-and-bones bodies: "For I know that my Redeemer lives, and He shall stand at last *on the earth*; and after my skin is destroyed, this I know that *in my flesh* I shall see God, whom I shall see for myself, and my eyes shall behold, and not another. How my heart yearns within me!" (Job 19:25–27 NKJV, italics mine).

Still, some of you may be struggling with a few seemingly contradictory passages in the Old Testament. Let's explore those before moving on to the New Testament's verses on the state of the dead.

CHAPTER 5

But What about These OT Passages?

A FEW PASSAGES IN the Old Testament have been interpreted (or taken out of context) to prove the dead are conscious. Context is so crucial because, as mentioned before, the Bible isn't always literal. It uses figurative, poetic, and prophetic language. Like a puzzle, students of the Bible have to carefully piece together the picture of truth without forcing a shape into a hole that does not fit.

Let's take a look at these few OT passages, in context, and in light of the other two C's: God's character and the consistency of the entire Bible.

Isaiah Chapter 14

Here's how Isaiah chapter 14 verses 3–11 read (NKJV):

> It shall come to pass in the day the Lord gives you rest from your sorrow, and from your fear and the hard bondage in which you were made to serve, that you will take up this proverb against the king of Babylon and say:
> "How the oppressor has ceased, The golden city ceased!
> The Lord has broken the staff of the wicked, The scepter of the rulers;
> He who struck the people in wrath with a continual stroke, He who ruled the nations in anger, Is persecuted and no one hinders.
> The whole earth is at rest and quiet; They break forth into singing.
> Indeed the cypress trees rejoice over you, And the cedars of Lebanon, Saying, 'Since you were cut down, No woodsman has come up against us.'

> Hell from beneath is excited about you, To meet you at your coming; It stirs up the dead for you. All the chief ones of the earth; It has raised up from their thrones All the kings of the nations.
>
> They all speak and say to you: 'Have you also become as weak as we? Have you become like us?
>
> Your pomp is brought down to Sheol, And the sound of your stringed instruments; The maggot is spread under you, And worms cover you.'"

In this ode, or proverb, the kings who were killed by the armies of Babylon are portrayed as alive in Sheol and pronouncing doom upon the current living king. They taunt him by saying how weak he has now become, like them—dead, with maggots beneath him and worms covering him. Even here, this is no image of tormenting fire. Nor is it implying there are immortal souls languishing in eternal consciousness. These kings wouldn't be on thrones if they were truly alive as spirits.

Here's a context clue that this is figurative and poetic, not literal: the trees rejoice and speak. The *trees* are the ones telling the king that the dead are stirred up to meet (welcome) him into sheol. We have to be reasonable!

Context is important. If you are going to take this passage literally—claim this proves the dead are conscious in sheol—then you have to believe trees speak—and in beautifully worded sentences (something I would love to see). Yet, respected scholars of the Bible will break this fundamental, logical rule of context and use this text as proof that hell is a place of punishment.

Ezekiel Chapters 31 and 32

The Bible uses a lot of poetic imagery when pronouncing judgments on nations; it's a common style. Here in Ezekiel—a book full of lots of symbolic imagery—we see in chapter 31 the Lord telling the prophet to speak to Pharaoh and say, "Whom are you like in your greatness?" (verse 2). He goes on to describe the nation of Assyria as a cedar with fine branches and high stature, full of birds' nests and beautiful with deep roots (verses 3–9). But then this tree merits God's wrath, and he allows it to be cut down, its boughs lying broken, and all the people who enjoyed the shade of the branches flee (verses 10–14).

Following is this pronouncement to Egypt's pharaoh (verses 15–18 NIV):

> This is what the Sovereign Lord says: On the day it was brought down to the realm of the dead I covered the deep springs with mourning for it; I held back its streams, and its abundant waters were restrained. Because of it I clothed Lebanon with gloom, and all the trees of the field withered away.
>
> I made the nations tremble at the sound of its fall when I brought it down to the realm of the dead [sheol] to be with those who go down to the pit [bowr]. Then all the trees of Eden, the choicest and best of Lebanon, the well-watered trees, were consoled in the earth below.
>
> They too, like the great cedar, had gone down to the realm of the dead, to those killed by the sword, along with the armed men who lived in its shade among the nations.
>
> Which of the trees of Eden can be compared with you in splendor and majesty? Yet you, too, will be brought down with the trees of Eden to the earth below; you will lie among the uncircumcised, with those killed by the sword. This is Pharaoh and all his hordes, declares the Sovereign Lord.

Here we see another poetic, figurative portrayal of this ruler going "down" to sheol to be with other soldiers in the pit. In Ezekiel 32:27, fallen men are described in sheol as lying with swords under their head and shields covering them. Not an image of fiery torture or heavenly bliss; instead, this poetry aptly portrays their bodies buried in the ground.

What Are "Shades" in the Old Testament?

The Hebrew word *rapha*, used eight times in the Old Testament, is translated as dead (seven times) and deceased (one time) in the KJV (Job 26:5; Ps 88:10; Prov 2:18; 9:18; 21:16; Isa 14:9; 26:14, 19).

It is sometimes interpreted to mean ghost or spirit of the dead. Shades are believed, so say ancient Hebrews, to live in hades, according to the Gesenuis Hebrew-Chaldee Lexicon. The German etymology led this Bible scholar "to deduce that the Hebrew sheol meant no more than 'a hollow and subterranean place . . . full of thick darkness, in which the shades of the dead are gathered together.'"[1] Those ancients expressed belief that these

---

1. Davis, "Heaven, Sheol, and Gehenna," 19–20.

shades were void of blood and were therefore "weak and languid like a sick person but not devoid of powers of mind, such as memory"[2]—kind of like a zombie.

Scholar Edmund Keller writes:

> Early Hebrew thoughts of life and death are strikingly similar to those of the Babylonians. Three legends indicate that people considered the nether world as a vast cavern in the heart of the earth, into which light of day never penetrates; its inhabitants sit in darkness, their food is dust and mud. In the legend of the Descent of Ishtar we learn that the shades of the dead glide about in silence; or if there is any sound, it is sorrowful mourning of the inhabitants. They live on the dust that surrounds them and drink murky water. There is no hope or affection—a joyless existence.[3]

The verse in Isaiah 14:9 speaks of the dead as being "roused" to meet the king. As this study explains, *sleep* is a euphemism for death and the condition of the dead. If a spirit were immortal and always conscious, it would not need to be roused.

However, in Isaiah 26:14, we see another example of parallelism. The verse reads: "They are dead, they will not live; they are *rephaim* [deceased KJV, ASV, and NKJV; shades ESV and NRSV; departed spirits CSB and NASB], they will not arise." *Dead* parallels *rephaim*. "Not live" parallels "not arise." The matching pairs mean the same thing in parallelism.

To drive home the point that these rephaim are plain dead, the rest of the verse says, "Therefore you have punished and destroyed them [brought them to ruin]" (NKJV).

The Hebrew word *shamad* means to destroy, bring to naught, overthrow, perish, and pluck down. Nothing to indicate a conscious existence remains. Sorry, no zombies.

The Medium of Endor

This is a favorite passage of those who want to prove that the dead are disembodied spirits that, for some reason, are hanging around the earth and influence the living in some way.

---

2. Micou, *Basic Ideas*, 256.
3. Keller, "Hebrew Thoughts," 16.

Hell No

Let's read this passage at 1 Samuel 28:3–20 NKJV, then take a close look at it (yes, it's long, but the context is important—be sure to read the rest of the chapter too):

> Now Samuel had died, and all Israel had lamented for him and buried him in Ramah, in his own city. And Saul had put the mediums and the spiritists out of the land.
>
> Then the Philistines gathered together, and came and encamped at Shunem. So Saul gathered all Israel together, and they encamped at Gilboa. When Saul saw the army of the Philistines, he was afraid, and his heart trembled greatly. And when Saul inquired of the Lord, the Lord did not answer him, either by dreams or by Urim or by the prophets.
>
> Then Saul said to his servants, "Find me a woman who is a medium, that I may go to her and inquire of her."
>
> And his servants said to him, "In fact, there is a woman who is a medium at En Dor."
>
> So Saul disguised himself and put on other clothes, and he went, and two men with him; and they came to the woman by night. And he said, "Please conduct a séance for me, and bring up for me the one I shall name to you."
>
> Then the woman said to him, "Look, you know what Saul has done, how he has cut off the mediums and the spiritists from the land. Why then do you lay a snare for my life, to cause me to die?"
>
> And Saul swore to her by the Lord, saying, "As the Lord lives, no punishment shall come upon you for this thing."
>
> Then the woman said, "Whom shall I bring up for you?"
>
> And he said, "Bring up Samuel for me."
>
> When the woman saw Samuel, she cried out with a loud voice. And the woman spoke to Saul, saying, "Why have you deceived me? For you are Saul!"
>
> And the king said to her, "Do not be afraid. What did you see?"
>
> And the woman said to Saul, "I saw a spirit ascending out of the earth."
>
> So he said to her, "What is his form?"
>
> And she said, "An old man is coming up, and he is covered with a mantle." And Saul perceived that it was Samuel, and he stooped with his face to the ground and bowed down.
>
> Now Samuel said to Saul, "Why have you disturbed me by bringing me up?"

> And Saul answered, "I am deeply distressed; for the Philistines make war against me, and God has departed from me and does not answer me anymore, neither by prophets nor by dreams. Therefore I have called you, that you may reveal to me what I should do."
>
> Then Samuel said: "So why do you ask me, seeing the LORD has departed from you and has become your enemy? And the LORD has done for himself as He spoke by me. For the LORD has torn the kingdom out of your hand and given it to your neighbor, David. Because you did not obey the voice of the LORD nor execute his fierce wrath upon Amalek, therefore the LORD has done this thing to you this day. Moreover the LORD will also deliver Israel with you into the hand of the Philistines. And tomorrow you and your sons will be with me. The LORD will also deliver the army of Israel into the hand of the Philistines."
>
> Immediately Saul fell full length on the ground, and was dreadfully afraid because of the words of Samuel. And there was no strength in him, for he had eaten no food all day or all night.

Here we see King Saul desperate for instruction, so he breaks God's law and seeks out a fortune-teller, which is forbidden—punishable under the Law by death (Lev 20:6, 27), of which Saul was very well aware (and hence why he snuck incognito to Endor to do this). Even this woman knew it was unlawful, but he assured her she wouldn't be punished for her crime.

She conjures up a "spirit," and Saul determines it's Samuel. This spirit chastises the king for disobeying God, then pronounces his doom.

Because of this account about a medium, many claim this is proof that the dead are still alive (but why Samuel's "ghost" would be available on call from "below" and not up in some happy heaven, they don't say).

Here's why this passage doesn't hold water.

First, consistency: it's wholly inconsistent with what the Old Testament teaches about the state of the dead, which, as we've explored, is nonexistence. Samuel, after he died, was dead—he no longer existed, and he still doesn't. He will be resurrected on the "day" when Christ calls the dead—the righteous and the unrighteous—from the grave. Samuel is "resting" along with the prophet Daniel, who was told to rest until that future time when he will be called back to life (Dan 12:13).

Second, since it was forbidden on penalty of death to consult a medium—one of the reasons Saul was condemned to die prematurely (1 Chr 10:13-14)—God would not use such a channel to send a message to Saul. Verse 6 states that God refused to speak to Saul (which is why he sought out the medium). So how could anyone then presume to believe that God changed his mind suddenly and decided to use a forbidden method to speak to Saul, conjuring up a "disembodied spirit" when Saul knew full well that there was no such thing? Saul was not only desperate but often, to my mind, irrational and impulsive in moments of desperation to the *n*th degree. Go read the chapters in the Bible that tell the story of his crazy behavior (book of 1 Samuel).

Leviticus states these mediums consult "familiar spirits" (Lev 19:31; cf. Isa 8:19). If these are not "spirits" from God, then they must be evil spirits, demons, who are to be shunned. If God wanted us to talk to our dead loved ones, he wouldn't have so vehemently forbidden a practice that claimed to be able to do just that.

Third, the medium said she saw "a god [Hebrew: *elohim*] coming up from the earth"—a word sometimes used for false gods, not just the Creator (see Gen 35:2; Exod 12:12). And the "god" was wearing clothes. Why would a disembodied spirit need clothes? one might wonder.

Fourth, if Samuel, being a holy and righteous man, had truly died and his immortal soul went somewhere, he surely wouldn't be in "hell" or a place where Saul would "join him" in death. One would think, following this fallacious reasoning, that Samuel would be in heaven and Saul would go to "hell"—hence the two wouldn't end up hanging together for eternity (1 Sam 28:19). Remember, the "spirit of Samuel" didn't complain that Saul had brought him "down" from his happy heavenly cloud; instead, he complained, "Why have you brought me *up*?" (from sheol).

I hope this gives you pause if you ever consider consulting a fortune-teller. While we are not under Levitical Law, God's warning was not for a frivolous reason. Consulting mediums opens you up to demonic influence. Beware. This is exactly what happened to Saul, and he paid the price.

I also hope you can see how relying on the Bible's consistency, keeping Scripture in context, and considering God's unchanging nature leads to a simple and clear explanation of the condition of the dead as described in the Old Testament.

The Transfiguration of Jesus

In three gospel accounts in the New Testament, we read about a peculiar event that occurs, and although this chapter you are currently reading is discussing the condition of the dead that's presented in the Old Testament, it's pertinent to take a look at this now, especially since we've learned that the dead are not in existence anywhere and, hence, cannot appear to humans on the earth—no exceptions.

Let me set the stage. It's shortly before the end of Jesus's time here on earth. Jesus has just told his disciples he is going to be killed, and no doubt that has rattled their faith:

> From that time on Jesus began to explain to his disciples that he must go to Jerusalem and suffer many things at the hands of the elders, the chief priests and the teachers of the law, and that he must be killed and on the third day be raised to life.
> Peter took him aside and began to rebuke him. "Never, Lord!" he said. "This shall never happen to you!"
> Jesus turned and said to Peter, "Get behind me, Satan! You are a stumbling block to me; you do not have in mind the concerns of God, but merely human concerns." (Matt 17:21–23 NIV. Compare the account at Luke 9:22.)

Six days earlier, Jesus hints that something powerful is going to occur, no doubt intended to boost their faith and help them get through the emotional ordeal of the crucifixion. His followers are going to scatter, and their faith will be sorely tried. Jesus wants to ensure the foundling church does not get snuffed out by Satan (Luke 22:31). He tells them, "Truly I tell you, some who are standing here will not taste death before they see that the kingdom of God has come with power" (Mark 9:1 NIV). Matthew 16:28 words it this way: "before they see the Son of Man coming in his kingdom."

Here's what transpires the following week:

> And after six days Jesus took with him Peter and James, and John his brother, and led them up a high mountain by themselves. And he was transfigured before them, and his face shone like the sun, and his clothes became white as light. And behold, there appeared to them Moses and Elijah, talking with him. And Peter said to Jesus, "Lord, it is good that we are here. If you wish, I will make three tents here, one for you and one for Moses and one for Elijah." He was still speaking when, behold, a bright cloud overshadowed them, and a voice from the cloud said, "This is my beloved Son, with whom I am well pleased; listen to him." When the disciples heard this, they fell on their faces and were terrified. But Jesus came and touched them, saying, "Rise, and have no fear." And when they lifted up their eyes, they saw no one but Jesus only.
> And as they were coming down the mountain, Jesus commanded them, "Tell no one the vision, until the Son of Man is raised from the dead." And the disciples asked him, "Then why do

the scribes say that first Elijah must come?" He answered, "Elijah does come, and he will restore all things. But I tell you that Elijah has already come, and they did not recognize him, but did to him whatever they pleased. So also the Son of Man will certainly suffer at their hands." Then the disciples understood that he was speaking to them of John the Baptist. (Matt 17:1–13 ESV)

Jesus plainly states they saw a vision, and the disciples don't contest that fact. They know that the dead are dead; Moses (representing the Law) and Elijah (representing the prophets) had long ago been buried and are sleeping with their forefathers, and those two "apparitions" appear as if to confirm Jesus's post-resurrection words: "This is what I told you while I was still with you: Everything must be fulfilled that is written about me in the Law of Moses, the Prophets and the Psalms" (Luke 24:44 NIV). This understanding of the condition of the dead is precisely why they asked about the prophecy foretelling the coming of Elijah and what that meant symbolically, and Jesus answered that "Elijah" had indeed come.

Malachi the prophet foretold an "Elijah" that would pave the way for the Messiah, and that prophet was embodied in the person of John the Baptist. "Behold, I will send you Elijah the prophet before the great and awesome day of the Lord comes. And he will turn the hearts of fathers to their children and the hearts of children to their fathers, lest I come and strike the land with a decree of utter destruction" (Mal 4:5 ESV).

Peter confirms the purpose of the vision decades later when he writes this in his letter:

> For we were not making up clever stories when we told you about the powerful coming of our Lord Jesus Christ. We saw his majestic splendor with our own eyes when he received honor and glory from God the Father. The voice from the majestic glory of God said to him, "This is my dearly loved Son, who brings me great joy." We ourselves heard that voice from heaven when we were with him on the holy mountain. Because of that experience, we have even greater confidence in the message proclaimed by the prophets. (2 Pet 1:16–19 NLT)

He mentions nothing about the ancient prophets being alive or existing in heaven as spirits, nor that the vision portrayed them in heaven; rather, it showed them on earth, alongside Jesus.

The Greek word for *vision* is *horama* (Strong's G3705), which is consistently used in all twelve NT instances in the way we understand the word today. A vision is a supernatural depiction—not reality. Jesus didn't tell his three companions they'd actually seen Elijah and Moses raised from the dead and in spirit bodies. He said plainly they'd experienced a divinely given vision (for examples of this use of horama, see Acts 9:12; 10:3, 17, 19; 12:9; 16:9).

The word used for *appeared* ("There appeared to them Moses and Elijah") is *optanomai* (Strong's G3700), which conveys the sense of behold, to look at, experience, allow oneself to be seen—nothing that indicates these men were actually there.

Consider this too: since it was unlawful to attempt to speak to dead spirits, Jesus would have been breaking the Mosaic Law if he'd actually summoned these "spirits" and then would have not kept the Law perfectly—which was a requirement of the unblemished Lamb of God foretold to take away the sins of the world.

One might argue that Jesus raised them from the dead in order to speak to them, but, if he had, where did those prophets then go? Back to the dust again, to await the resurrection? The reasonable course is to accept Jesus's own words that this was only a vision and not read into it more than is there—and anything that contradicts the body of Scripture.

This vision helped bolster his disciples' faith, as they saw a glimpse of what it will be like in Jesus's kingdom. Receiving a powerful vision of the promised resurrection of the faithful, those witnesses to the transfiguration—which featured God's own voice confirming Jesus's authority ("Listen to him")—experienced something powerful and faith-strengthening that they no doubt reflected on throughout the years of their lives. We may not know why Jesus chose those specific three followers to see him transfigured, but he knew why, and clearly he believed it was important they experience this amazing and magnificent vision.

Let's now examine what the New Testament says about the condition of those who've died—just in case you're inclined to think that God, his pronouncements, and the laws governing his creation changed with the arrival of Jesus on earth.

CHAPTER 6

The State of the Dead in the New Testament

*The doctrine of eternal torment actually rests on just four "core" texts. . . .
It should concern all Bible students to note how few proof-texts can be
cited in support of eternal torment.*
—Ralph G. Bowles, priest and biblical scholar[1]

INTERESTINGLY, THE NEW TESTAMENT has few verses pertaining to the state of the dead. The Jews already knew the dead were gone, no longer in existence, and while the religious sect of the Sadducees did not believe in the resurrection—unlike the Pharisees—they did accept the established teaching of sheol being the place where the dead go and are, plainly stated, dead (which is the reason for the cute little mnemonic about the Sadducees: "That's why they are *sad, you see*"—sad because they have no future hope).

I mentioned how the Jews during the four-hundred-year period of "silence" from God before the arrival of the Messiah (called the intertestamental period) were greatly influenced by the culture around them. The Hellenistic Jews grew to accept many of the Greek beliefs, such as immortality of the soul and the concept of an underworld in which these souls went either to heaven or a torturous hell immediately after death.

Jesus, fully aware of this pollution of their Jewish belief system, sometimes utilized these erroneous beliefs to drive home truth.

In total, there are eleven verses in the New Testament that refer to hades—which is the Greek word equivalent to the Hebrew sheol—and in

---

1. Bowles, "Revelation 14:11," 32, 33.

ten of those verses the King James Version of the Bible translates hades as hell (the other lone reference is translated as grave).

The word *gehenna* is used twelve times as well, but we'll look at those in a bit.

Jesus himself used the word hades only three times. So let's start there.

"You Will Be Brought Down to Hades"

In Matthew 11:23 we read Jesus's words: "And you, Capernaum, will you be exalted to heaven? You will be brought down to Hades" (ESV).

What's the context here? Verse 20 tells us Jesus "began to rebuke" the cities in which he did powerful works but whose citizens refused to repent. Jesus cries woe to them, then uses this figurative language to warn them of their punishment. Not the individual people but the cities themselves, personified, are told that rather than be "exalted to heaven" (nothing said here about immortal souls actually going to heaven), Capernaum will be brought down to hades.

As is wholly consistent with so many Old Testament verses, hades is portrayed as the deepest place on earth—under the ground, far from God in heaven "above," the realm of the dead (see Amos 9:2–3; Job 11:7–9). Hence why Jesus used the phrase "brought down." It is understandable that Jesus would also use this type of description, being that he often referenced the Hebrew Law and the writings of the prophets.

The second use of hades is in the parable of the Rich Man and Lazarus, explained further in this chapter.

The third use of hades is in Matthew 16:18, in which Jesus states: "On this rock I will build my church, and the gates of hades shall not prevail against it."

The Bible, as well as ancient Jewish writings, uses "gates of death" as a figurative way to describe sheol. Job writes: "Have the gates of death been revealed to you, or have you seen the gates of deep darkness?" (Job 38:17 KJV). Those "gates" could not prevail over Jesus's kingdom because Jesus would soon conquer death for all time and be given the keys to death and hades (Rev 1:18). With those figurative keys, he can lock those "gates" so that they are shut forever after they "give up their dead" (Rev 20:13).

Beautiful imagery, but surely not teaching there is a conscious place of torment for the wicked in hades. In fact, hades itself is thrown into the lake of fire at the end of the thousand-year reign of Christ on earth, which would make no sense if it were a literal place of fire (fire being thrown into fire to be destroyed?).

The Bible promises "death will be no more." Period. That means death and hades are destroyed in that symbolic lake, never to return. That's true victory!

6 "Controversial" Passages in the New Testament

Veering off from hades and gehenna a moment, we should take a look at six other passages often cited as proof of instant reward or punishment upon death. In Luke 23:42–43, Jesus promised the thief hanging on the cross alongside him that he would join him in paradise.

Without getting too geeky, be aware that the phrase (which translated literally reads: "Truly to you I say today with me you will be in paradise"), in placing the word *today* (*semeron*) between "I say" (*lego*) and "you will be with me" (*ese*), it means *today* could apply to either verb.

People assume when Jesus says to the thief hanging alongside him, "Truly I tell you today you will be with me in paradise," he means the thief was going to go to paradise with Jesus *that very day*. That would be impossible.

First off, Jesus died, was buried, and did not come back to life (he was flat-out dead) until the third day (1 Cor 15:3–4). There was no paradise for Jesus or the thief to go to on that dark day in the first century because paradise exists in a future time. He won't be in paradise until he brings the kingdom from heaven to earth, where he says he will again eat and drink with his faithful followers. And the thief first has to go to "sleep" until the day Jesus resurrects everyone—the righteous and unrighteous. So, certainly, if you were to add punctuation to that verse, it would read, "Truly I tell you *today*, . . . you will be with me in paradise [sometime in the future]."

Translators put the comma before the word *today* solely to support their theological teaching that the dead instantly get rewarded (or punished) at the moment of death, which is contrary to all Scripture.

Some like to argue that only Christ's *body* was buried in the grave but his soul went to heaven (presuming the Bible teaches humans—including the man Jesus—have "souls" hidden inside them). If that were true, why did Jesus tell Mary after he was resurrected: "Do not hold on to me, for I have not yet ascended to the Father" (John 20:17 NIV)? Here Jesus plainly said he hadn't returned to heaven yet, and that's because he had been dead. Not alive. He wasn't brought back to life until the third day. This isn't complicated, folks!

Here are the other five troublesome passages, and we'll examine them carefully:

1. Luke 16:19–31: A symbolic depiction of "death" in the parable of the Rich Man and Lazarus.
2. Philippians 1:23: Paul expressed his "desire to depart and be with Christ."
3. 2 Corinthians 5:1–10: Paul uses a metaphor of houses to convey his wish to "be away from the body and at home with the Lord."
4. Revelation 6:9–11: Martyred souls under the altar of God cry out for their blood to be avenged.
5. Romans 2:5–9: Paul warns of the day of wrath, which is wrought with fiery judgment.

Let's take a look at each of these in context, keeping in mind the passages must be consistent with the entire Bible and with God's unchangeable character.

The Rich Man Suffering in Hellfire

I once had a discussion with a man who attended church with me, and I logically tried to explain to him how the Bible did not support the teaching of eternal hellfire. I shared many verses with him, but, ultimately, he threw up his hands and said something like, "Well, I just can't agree with you because Jesus made it clear the wicked will suffer in hellfire in the parable of the Rich Man and Lazarus."

Even though I showed him verses that explained how Jesus spoke in parables, which are symbolic and not literal (that in itself should be enough of a basis), and I pointed out how ludicrous it would be to support a belief of eternal torment on a story about one unnamed man who is tortured merely because he was rich, he wouldn't budge.

There are so many facets of this parable found at Luke 16:19–31 that prove it is not literal, and when understanding Jesus's audience and the context of his telling this parable, I hope it will become clear to you just what Jesus is really talking about here. So let's disassemble this parable (please read it first).

The victim in this parable is an unnamed rich man. He is never accused of committing any particular sin, which, if literally applied, would imply every rich person in the world should expect to burn in hell. In comparison, the character Lazarus isn't portrayed as righteous or deserving of reward. Jews of Jesus's day knew the Law and understood all were sinners and that no one could be declared righteous unless they kept the Law perfectly. They also knew the condition of the dead from their sacred writings from God—that every person who dies returns to the dust, in sheol. So Jesus's listeners would never take this parable literally. Context!

Not only is it ludicrous to think someone in hell (the pit, the grave) is conscious, it is more so to think they could observe someone in heaven, speak across the "chasm," or be relieved from the pain of fire eating their flesh by a mere drop of water.

The other big problem we face is if we insist on taking this parable literally, we have to take every parable Jesus shared literally. Yet Psalm 78:2 is referenced when it's said in Matthew 13:34–35 that Jesus "spoke all these things to the crowd in parables; he did not say anything to them without using a parable. So was fulfilled what was spoken through the prophet" (NIV).

When his disciples asked why he used parables, Jesus explained.

> I speak to them in parables, because seeing they do not see, and hearing they do not hear, nor do they understand. And in them the prophecy of Isaiah is fulfilled, which says: 'Hearing you will hear and shall not understand, and seeing you will see and not perceive; for the hearts of this people have grown dull. Their ears are hard of hearing, and their eyes they have closed, lest they should see with their eyes and hear with their ears, lest they should understand with their hearts and turn, so that I should heal them.'" (verses 13–14 NKJV)

Should we be surprised that so many people misinterpret this highly symbolic parable?

By looking at the context of this parable, it helps with understanding its purpose and audience. Right before Jesus told this parable, the religious leaders were raging over Jesus drawing sinners to hear him—and not only that, he was consorting with them, eating with them. No doubt they were jealous of his fame and his ability to do miracles (which they couldn't do) as well as hated the way Jesus exposed their hypocrisy in no vague terms.

Jesus shared some parables that highlighted God's love for the lost, then followed with his powerful damning parable of the unfaithful steward (Luke 16:1–13). Luke tells us the Pharisees were lovers of money (verse 14), so they, no doubt, would have assumed Jesus was alluding to them as the *collective* rich man in his next parable.

In the parable, the rich man is wearing robes that imply the priesthood, and he eats sumptuously. Figuratively, the Jews—God's holy people, given the sacred pronouncements of God—enjoyed a spiritual feast, but their leaders became arrogant and selfish (Rom 3:2).

Lazarus is described as a beggar who longed to be fed from the crumbs of the rich man's table, which is an apt description of the Gentiles at that time, described by Paul in Ephesians 2:12 as separated from God and having no hope. It was common for Jews of Jesus's day to call Gentiles "unclean dogs." Even Jesus took advantage of this view in how he spoke to the Gentile woman asking for healing in Mark 7:24–30.

In the parable, when Lazarus dies, the angels carry him not to God's presence but into Abraham's bosom (and the Jews, of course, believed Abraham was "sleeping with his fathers" in sheol awaiting a future resurrection). Lazarus is not buried, but the rich man was—in hades (verse 23). Right there is another bit of proof this is a parable because hades is a burial place, not a fiery hell.

What, then, is this parable all about?

Simply, Lazarus represents the Gentiles and the rich man the Jewish nation. This is a story about two groups and their standing with God. Death is a symbol of transition, and so, in this parable, what changes?

The rich man supposedly had favor in his life, whereas the poor man did not. But then, a shift occurs. Now the poor man is elevated to the highest favor (which is what being in Abraham's bosom implies—cf. John 13:23). What follows Jesus's death is the door opening to the Gentiles to come into a favored position that previously was only available to the Jews. They would no longer be strangers but "fellow citizens with the saints and members of the household of God" (Eph 2:19 NKJV). They would only need to believe in Christ to be saved, freely forgiven, and welcomed, but Paul warned sternly in the book of Romans (see chapter 11 specifically) that the Jews, if they were not careful, could be cut off from favor and discarded. Gentiles could take their place, and the rejected Jews would suffer the consequences. Indeed, Jesus told those "rich men" of Israel, "I tell you, many will come from east and west and will eat with Abraham and Isaac and Jacob in the kingdom of heaven, while the heirs of the kingdom will be thrown into the outer darkness, where there will be weeping and gnashing of teeth" (Matt 8:11–12 NRSV).

Seeing themselves "kicked out of the kingdom" they had long assumed they were entitled to would be the "torment" spoken of in the parable. You can imagine how furious the religious leaders of Jesus's time were to hear this parable and understand Jesus was talking about their rejection.

CHAPTER 7

What Do the NT Writers Say?

MOVING ON FROM JESUS, let's tackle those four other controversial passages about the condition of the dead mentioned in the previous chapter, keeping in mind these New Testament writers were all Jews and knew the sacred pronouncements of God given to the nation of Israel through Moses and the prophets.

This next passage can be a bit tricky, however. Paul expresses "having a desire to depart and to be with Christ" (Phil 1:23 NIV). He prefaces that sentiment with these words:

> For to me, to live is Christ and to die is gain. If I am to go on living in the body, this will mean fruitful labor for me. Yet what shall I choose? I do not know! I am torn between the two." (verses 21–22)

Those verses are often used to "prove" Paul had a heavenly hope. Another verse often referred to, to prove Paul is in heaven now, is 2 Corinthians 5:8, where he writes he is "willing rather to be absent from the body and to be present with the Lord" (KJV).

Since we know the righteous will be resurrected on earth and live there forever, how are we to understand what he means?

If you believe you immediately go to heaven when you die, you would presume one action follows the other without a break in time—departing "the body" and instantly being "present with the Lord." Yet, it would be inconsistent for Paul to believe this when, viewing his own words, he preached that Christ would return to earth and reign here for a thousand years (see also Heb 9:28; Acts 17:31). Second Timothy 4:1 is just one place in which Paul reminds believers that Jesus will judge both the living and the dead at "his appearing and his kingdom" (KJV).

57

The simple and true answer to where and when Paul expected to be with Jesus is here on earth, when the Lord would "appear" again.

The NT writers spoke often of Christ's return (as did Jesus numerous times in the gospels). In 2 Timothy 4:7–8, Paul speaks of finishing his course after fighting a good fight of faith, and that, because of his faithfulness, "there is laid up for me a crown of righteousness which the Lord, the righteous judge, shall give me *at that day* and not to me only, but unto all them also that love his *appearing*" (KJV, italics mine).

Paul's crown of glory (1 Pet 5:4) is "laid up" for him in heaven, as are all the crowns of the faithful (Rev 2:10), and will be given to him not upon his death but upon Jesus's "appearing." Appearing where? Jesus is now in heaven, so his appearing clearly means his return to earth. So this is no "instant ticket to heaven" to be with Jesus. This is waiting in death for the day of resurrection (in which those in Christ will rise first), when Jesus "appears" and not earlier.

The writer of Hebrews, at the end of chapter 11, makes an interesting statement about the many "hall of fame" faithful men and women he's just listed and described: "These were all commended for their faith, yet none of them received what had been promised, since God had planned something better for us so that only together with us would they be made perfect" (Heb 11:30–40 NIV). This reiterates the consistent Bible truth that every single person who's lived has not yet been given their "reward." All the blessings God promised those faithful are to be given upon their resurrection—alongside ("together") with the apostles and disciples of Jesus's day.

Remember: if you believe the righteous go to heaven when they die, then it negates the consistent Bible teaching that the righteous will be resurrected, along with the unrighteous, in that day in which Jesus will come to rule the earth for a thousand years.

Paul had a longing to be with Jesus and attain that resurrection of the dead (Phil 3:11) and included himself when he said, "We must all appear before the judgment seat of Christ" (2 Cor 5:10), when Christ will judge everyone who's ever lived "at his appearing and his Kingdom" (2 Tim 4:1 KJV—see also Col 3:4).

In other words, being "present with" the Lord was/is predicated on Christ *first returning and raising the dead*. He knew once he died, he would "sleep" in Christ (1 Thess 4:14) and that he would wake out of sleep (John 11:11) in a new immortal body and have an honored place (wearing that glorious crown) in Christ's kingdom here on earth (Rev 20:6). Jesus directly told his apostles that, in the resurrection, when he sits on his throne, they would also sit on twelve thrones. There is no reason to believe any of his apostles or disciples thought they would go to heaven and the thrones will be there.

But, you might argue, Jesus told his disciples while still alive on earth that he would soon leave them, promising, "My father's house has many rooms... And if I go and prepare a place for you, I will come back and take you to be with me that you also may be where I am" (John 14:3 NIV).

Stop and think a moment. What "house" would the disciples live in, with Jesus? If the apostles were promised to sit on thrones with him, where is this to be? The Bible clearly says it's on earth. No sense having Christ ruling on earth for a thousand years but his apostles sitting on thrones in heaven. "And just as My Father has granted Me a kingdom, I grant you that you may eat and drink at My table in My kingdom, and you will sit on thrones judging the twelve tribes of Israel" (Luke 22:29–30 KJV).

These are the same thrones in Revelation 20:4, where it speaks of those who were martyred for Jesus and now have authority to judge. They are said, right after Satan is bound and sealed in an abyss for a thousand years, that they only *then* "came to life and reigned with Christ for a thousand years." Not the moment they died. Not starting back in the first century up till now. Everyone is dead, in the grave (sheol), until Jesus raises them. The dead in Christ are raised first (more on that later) in what's called "the first resurrection."

So when Jesus says he's off to prepare a place for them and will come back, he doesn't say "to take you all to heaven to live there with me." He says "take you to be with me that you also may *be where I am*" (my italics). Where exactly will Jesus be when he resurrects them? He will *already have returned to rule on earth* (see later chapter on Jesus coming on the clouds in his return). The heavenly city of New Jerusalem "comes down from heaven" to earth (Rev 21:2). Whatever "rooms" Jesus has prepared for his faithful followers in that city not made by human hands, they will be rooms here on earth.

Jesus spoke in Luke 13:28–29 how Abraham and Isaac and Jacob— yes, even all the prophets who lived in the past—would sit in a place in the kingdom of God. These faithful ones of old were promised a kingdom *on earth*. They didn't receive the promises God gave them on earth (Heb 11:13); instead, they "saw them afar off." Did the writer of Hebrews mean heaven?

No. Because those men of old were not promised heaven. They were promised land on earth—literal land they would inherit. And hadn't yet inherited it—but saw it "afar off," in the future. Romans 4:13 says that Abraham would be "heir of the world," this world. Not heaven. Hebrews says that all believers in Christ are heirs of the same promise! That means . . . all of us, like Abraham, are heirs of this world, this planet.

God didn't change his promise. God doesn't negate his word. God never fails to fulfill what he promises. He promised Abraham that one day he would have it as his possession (see Acts 7:1–5). It would be a "heaven*ly*" country—*like* heaven but *not* heaven (Heb 11:6). If he took all these folks to heaven without giving them their promised land, God would have lied and proven unfaithful.

As with Abraham, the prophet Daniel was not promised a place in heaven but was told to rest until "the end of the days," when he would get his "allotted inheritance" (Dan 12:13 NIV). What was that inheritance? Daniel spoke of a kingdom "under the whole heaven" (not *in* heaven—Dan 7:13–14 KJV).

King David was also said to have died and been buried and had not "ascended into the heavens" (Acts 2:34). Pay attention to the fact that the word *yet* is *not* to be found in that phrase. Context shows David lying in the grave to that day is contrasted to the amazing truth that the man Jesus *did* ascend to heaven—an astonishing idea to people who would never have thought that possible. Remember: the writer of Hebrews says none of the faithful who lived before him had been made perfect yet (if they went to heaven, that would not be true—Heb 11:32). Consistency and context—that's how you get to the truth.

You'd Think Paul Would Have Mentioned It

Paul never once in the NT mentions anything about the body being reunited with the soul in the resurrection. Surely he would have said something about it, rather than speak about those "asleep in Christ" waking at some future appointed day. In his extensive discussions on the resurrection, in 1 Thessalonians chapter 4 and 1 Corinthians chapter 15, there is no mention of a conscious soul that survives death and is then sent to either heaven or hellfire. In fact, never—not once in any of Paul's writings—does he talk about hellfire. Rather, he mentions death, perish, and destroy when talking about the fate of the wicked. He says of enemies of the cross: "their end is destruction"—not torment forever (Phil 3:19—see also Rom 2:12; 1 Cor 3:17; Phil 1:28).

Stop and think about that. Paul covers a plethora of topics in his thirteen epistles. If the majority of humans on earth throughout all the centuries was destined to be sent, as immortal souls, to a place of burning, endless torment, it might have crossed his mind to mention it. You think?

When Paul appears before Felix in Acts 24:25, there is scant mention of the judgment to come. Surely if Felix's soul was in peril of eternal torment, Paul would have felt it important to mention. Also in Acts chapters 10 and 17, in Paul's warnings to the crowds, he tells them there will be a future day of judgment in which Jesus will judge those living and dead, but nowhere is a burning hellfire mentioned. Did he just forget to tell them about it? Did he think it wasn't important? I doubt that was the case—rather, he didn't mention it because he didn't believe in hellfire and eternal torment. Why would he? He certainly wasn't taught it in his intense Jewish studies at the feet of the prestigious rabbi Gamaliel (Acts 22:3).

The Other New Testament Writers

And what about the other NT writers of epistles? Surely Peter, one of the twelve apostles who spent three years alongside Jesus—talking, sleeping, eating, listening to their Savior (though I wonder, sometimes, how well Peter listened)—would warn of such punishment in his two letters. But while he uses symbolic language to describe the end of this human system, saying, "The day of the Lord will come like a thief. The heavens will disappear with a roar; the elements will be destroyed by fire, and the earth and everything done in it will be laid bare. Since everything will be destroyed in this way, what kind of people ought you to be?" (2 Pet 3:10–11 NIV), we know that neither the literal heavens nor God's domain will be actually destroyed. And even though fire is mentioned here, its purpose—clearly symbolic—is so that "everything done in it will be laid bare." Not used as a punishment.

Note how he uses the expression "fiery ordeal" in 1 Peter 4:12 (NIV—cf. Rev 18:9, 18)—the same Greek word *pyrosis* is used, and these are the only usages in the New Testament.

James, Jesus's half-brother, in his letter gives plenty of warnings. But they are of death, destruction, being fattened for slaughter, and riches consuming flesh like fire (1:15; 4:12; 5:3, 5, 19). In alignment with the basic fact often reiterated in the NT, James tells us that "sin when it is full-grown brings forth death" (Jas. 1:15 KJV)—because the price one pays (the wages) for being sinful is death and only death. To bookend this, James closes his epistle by telling believers to admonish one another because "whoever turns a sinner from the error of their way will save them from death" (5:20 NIV). Not eternal torment.

The apostle John in his letters says nothing about hellfire but simply makes the contrast of two possible fates—life and death. In 1 John 3:14–15 (NKJV) he says, "We know that we have passed from death to life, because we love the brethren. He who does not love his brother abides in death. Whoever hates his brother is a murderer, and you know that no murderer has eternal life abiding in him." And in the vision John is given in Revelation, the twenty-four elders proclaim: "The time has come for judging the dead … and for destroying those who destroy the earth" (11:18 NIV). I find this passage one of the most convincing of the Bible's divine authorship because only in recent decades have humans not only had the potential to destroy the planet (with nuclear warfare) but also have been actually threatening the future existence of the planet. We humans are now destroying the entire earth, and since this is Christ's possession and inheritance, he will intervene before it's too late—by destroying (not tormenting in a hellfire) those whose wanton and greedy actions are threatening God's jewel of a home for mankind.

See how simple and clear this is? The choice is life or death. God urges us to choose life so we might live. Romans 6:23 tells us the wages of sin is death, "but the gift of God is eternal life in Christ Jesus our Lord" (NIV).

Instead of hoping to live in some nebulous spirit body in some unimaginable place "up there," we can rejoice in the comfort and confidence that this earth, which we were made from and for, will be our eternal home. It will be a "new earth"—no, not a new planet! The "old earth" was destroyed by the flood of Noah's day, but it's the same planet. Peter explains that just as the world *at that time* was "destroyed" by water, this world (society, system) of humankind will again be destroyed but this time by "fire" (read 2 Peter chapter 3).

We know the Bible uses fire as a symbol of complete annihilation, as it burns things to ash, leaving nothing salvageable (more on that, too, in a later chapter). We should be excited to spend eternity in this earth that "abideth forever" (Eccl 1:4 KJV)—the home of humankind, where, as God promised Noah, "While the earth remains, seedtime and harvest, cold and heat, summer and winter, day and night, shall not cease" (ESV). God has firmly established the earth to remain forever, orbiting our sun, season after beautiful season. And God's tent will forever reside with the humans he created.

What About Hebrews?

The writer of the letter to the Hebrews makes a statement in chapter 3 that seems to imply a heavenly calling for followers of Christ: "And so, dear brothers and sisters who belong to God and are partners with those called to heaven, think carefully about this Jesus whom we declare to be God's messenger and High Priest" (3:1 NLT). Let's tear this apart. Here are some other translations of the phrase in question:

> KJV/NKJV/NASB: "partakers of the heavenly calling"
> NIV/ESV: "who share in the/a heavenly calling"
> New English Translation: "partners in a heavenly calling"

Here's a typical explanation of this verse (this one by a man named Bruce Hurt, who has a religious website): "The writer [of Hebrews] thus demonstrates clearly the superiority of Christianity to Judaism. Judaism was an earthly calling with an earthly inheritance. Christianity is a spiritual and heavenly calling with a spiritual and heavenly inheritance. It is, therefore, far superior."[1]

I hope this makes you bristle. You should now understand how the Bible is one consistent whole and that God never changes. The idea that people who lived before Christ walked this earth would get an earthly inheritance, whereas believers in Jesus would get to go to heaven is nonsense. People pre-Christ didn't get "called" to earth; they already lived on earth. It isn't a calling. Judaism wasn't inferior to Christianity. His remark makes it sound, to me, that getting "earth" was a pathetic consolation prize instead of the glorious inheritance God designed and promised humans from the foundation of the world.

What Hebrews teaches us is that *Jesus* was superior, better than the high priests under the Mosaic Law. His sacrifice was greater, and all that came under the Law foreshadowed and typified the better covenant to come—one that could completely save and was also inclusive of Gentiles, not just Jews. But Judaism itself, the "religion" God gave his chosen people,

---

1. Hurt, "Hebrews 3:1–4 Commentary," section 2.

wasn't inferior. How could it be when Jesus himself was a Jew—a faithful Jew who practiced and kept the Law perfectly?

If we look at the actual Greek, here's what we find. The word for *partners* is the adjective *metochos*, which means a participant, a sharer, an associate. The image is not of one who is being called to heaven but partnering up with others who are. What about *heavenly calling*? The word for heavenly—*epouranios*—can mean heavenly regions, existing in heaven, or heavenly origin or nature. Paul in Philippians 3:14 speaks of this upward or heavenly calling he is striving for.

Thayer's Greek Lexicon has this: "a call, invitation: to a feast, in the N.T. everywhere in a technical sense, the divine invitation to embrace salvation in the kingdom of God, which is made especially through the preaching of the gospel."

Commentator David Guzik says, "Because Jesus is committed to bringing many sons to glory (Heb 2:10), we are partners in his heavenly calling."[2] Followers of Jesus are told they will rule as kings and priests in his kingdom—that's a partnership.

It sure looks like, for all intents and purposes, the writer of Hebrews is plainly stating that believers go to heaven. But since we know the entire Bible teaches otherwise, as do all the New Testament writers and Jesus, there has to be a nuance here we are missing.

The emphasis in the phrase is on the *sharing* or partnering with Jesus's heavenly calling. Since Jesus stated that no person has gone or will go to heaven except for himself (John 3:13), doesn't this interpretation make sense?

This invitation to share in Christ's kingdom, which comes down from heaven to bless earth's inhabitants, is something we long to be participating in. It doesn't mean we have to go up to heaven to share in this heavenly calling. In Revelation 22:17 we get this invitation: "The Spirit and the bride say, 'Come!' And let the one who hears say, 'Come!' Let the one who is thirsty come; and let the one who wishes take the free gift of the water of life" (NIV).

The Cambridge Greek Testament for Schools and Colleges makes an important point: "It is a heavenly calling because it comes from heaven (Hebrews 12:25), and is a call 'upwards' to heavenly things (Philippians 3:14) and to holiness (1 Thessalonians 4:7)."[3]

2. Guzik, "Hebrews 3," para. 1.
3. Cambridge Commentary, "Commentary on Hebrews," section 2.

Further in chapter 3 of Hebrews, the writer uses that same word for "partakers," saying "we have become partakers of Christ" (verse 14). But we don't become partakers by going to heaven; we do so "if we hold the beginning of our confidence steadfast to the end" (NKJV). That Greek word for *become (ginomai)* implies a completion: to be made, to come into existence, to receive. The passage doesn't say "we *will* become partakers of Christ *once we get to heaven.*" It says "we *have* become" partakers *if we continue faithful.* We can partake—and actually do so now—on earth by being faithful to Christ and thereby reaping the benefits of his heavenly calling.

Note, too, how the apostle Peter speaks of God's divine power making it possible for believers, by way of these "great and precious promises" of eternal life, to "be partakers of the divine nature" now—not later after we die (1 Pet 1:3–4 NKJV). It is by this partaking that we have escaped (past tense, not sometime in the future) the corruption in the world.

We don't need to go to heaven to share or partake in Jesus's heavenly calling. Keeping all Scripture in context and consistent with all other Bible teaching, it makes the most sense to dismiss this singular verse as proof that believers in Jesus will go live in heaven in some "spiritual form" after they die.

Flesh and Blood Cannot Inherit the Kingdom

An oft-quoted Scripture that some point to as proof of a heavenly reward for the righteous is 1 Corinthians 15:50. Paul lays out the topic in verse 35: "But someone will ask, 'How are the dead raised? With what kind of body will they come?'" (NIV).

He answers with (another) confirmation that every living thing, including humans, must first die (verse 36). Hebrews 9:27 says plainly, "It is appointed for men to die once." No human has ever been taken to heaven, and no person is exempt from dying. This is why the passage in Genesis about Enoch not seeing death "because God took him" cannot mean he didn't die (Gen 5:24). The writer of Hebrews helps us understand this incident by noting that by faith Enoch was taken away so that he did not *see* death, "and was not found, because God had taken him" (Heb 11:5 NKJV).

The Greek verb *horao* that is translated as "see" does not mean he didn't die. It means to see with the eyes or mind, to perceive, to experience. Because Enoch was righteous, "known as a person who pleased God" (NLT), God spared him any suffering or pain that humans generally experience in death throes. While God extended this particular kindness to him, who knows how many people throughout the millennia God has done likewise for? The Greek word used for "taken" means transpose, to transfer, or to change. Enoch was "transposed" or "transferred" in a moment from life to death without having to "see" death. It was a merciful act; perhaps Enoch had a painful ailment that would have caused him great agony for many years. We don't know the circumstance he was in.

A similar situation is seen with Elijah the prophet. Elijah tells his successor, Elisha, that if Elisha sees him taken away, he'll get a double portion of his mentor's spirit. "And as they still went on and talked, behold, chariots of fire and horses of fire separated the two of them. And Elijah went up by a whirlwind into heaven" (2 Kgs 2:11 ESV). Many claim this is proof God took Elijah to heaven so that he didn't actually die—just got his heavenly reward as a spirit being. Yet, years later, King Jehoram got a message from Elijah (2 Chr 21:12)—and, no, not from heaven. There are different heavens mentioned in the Bible—the atmospheric heaven being one of them, which is where you find whirlwinds. Though I imagine that whirlwind presented a wild ride for the retiring prophet, no doubt God deposited him somewhere safely on earth, out of Elisha's sight, so that those who had depended on the powerful prophet's divine utterances and powers would now defer to his successor (see 2 Kgs 2:15–18).

But let's return to Paul's letter to the Corinthians.

The key is in verse 37: "When you sow, you do not plant the body that will be, but just a seed, perhaps of wheat or of something else." After some discussion about the various types of "flesh" humans, animals, fish, and even heavenly bodies have, Paul expands this idea of a seed containing the essence or blueprint of the body.

Let's read this passage in context (verses 42–54 NIV):

> So will it be with the resurrection of the dead. The body that is sown is perishable, it is raised imperishable; it is sown in dishonor, it is raised in glory; it is sown in weakness, it is raised in power; it is sown a natural body, it is raised a spiritual body.
>
> If there is a natural body, there is also a spiritual body. So it is written: "The first man Adam became a living being"; the last Adam, a life-giving spirit. The spiritual did not come first, but the natural, and after that the spiritual. The first man was of the dust of the earth; the second man is of heaven. As was the earthly man, so are those who are of the earth; and as is the heavenly man, so also

> are those who are of heaven. And just as we have borne the image of the earthly man, so shall we bear the image of the heavenly man.
>
> I declare to you, brothers and sisters, that flesh and blood cannot inherit the kingdom of God, nor does the perishable inherit the imperishable. Listen, I tell you a mystery: We will not all sleep, but we will all be changed—in a flash, in the twinkling of an eye, at the last trumpet. For the trumpet will sound, the dead will be raised imperishable, and we will be changed. For the perishable must clothe itself with the imperishable, and the mortal with immortality. When the perishable has been clothed with the imperishable, and the mortal with immortality, then the saying that is written will come true: "Death has been swallowed up in victory."

Here we have established that corruption must be replaced with incorruption and mortality with immortality. The "flesh and blood" corruptible, perishable, mortal bodies cannot "inherit the kingdom" (note he did not say "cannot be allowed into heaven"). In 2 Corinthians 4:7 we read how we have this treasure of Christ, this precious knowledge of salvation, in earthen vessels (jars of clay). These breakable, perishable vessels could never inherit eternity; they're flawed, imperfect, full of sin. They will degrade and die unless they are raised up in a new form.

This understanding is further elucidated by Jesus's words in John chapter 3, where Jesus explains to a religious teacher that to inherit the kingdom, one must be "born again": "Very truly I tell you, no one can enter the kingdom of God unless they are born of water and the Spirit. Flesh gives birth to flesh, but the Spirit gives birth to spirit" (verses 5–6 NIV). What follows is the most famous of Jesus's words. He tells us that God loved the world so much, he gave his son to die as a payment for sin, so that "whoever believes in [Jesus] is not condemned, but whoever does not believe stands condemned already because they have not believed in the name of God's one and only Son" (verses 16 and 18).

When we believe, we become a "new creation." Hence, "the old has passed away; behold, the new has come" (2 Cor 5:17 ESV). This newness doesn't happen later, after we are resurrected; this occurs when we accept Jesus as our savior, which then gives us a new birth, and we are born again, of spirit. "For the spirit gives life" (2 Cor 2:6).

Romans 8:9–11 (ESV) says: "You, however, are not in the flesh but in the Spirit, if in fact the Spirit of God dwells in you. Anyone who does not have the Spirit of Christ does not belong to him. But if Christ is in you, although the body is dead because of sin, the Spirit is life because of righteousness. If the Spirit of him who raised Jesus from the dead dwells in you, he who raised Christ Jesus from the dead will also give life to your mortal bodies through his Spirit who dwells in you."

Paul told the Jews, who had formerly adhered to the Mosaic Law, "It doesn't matter whether we have been circumcised or not. What counts is whether we have been transformed into a new creation" (Gal 6:15 NLT). Romans 6:3–4 (NIV) says, "Or don't you know that all of us who were baptized into Christ Jesus were baptized into his death? We were therefore buried with him through baptism into death in order that, just as Christ was raised from the dead through the glory of the Father, we too may live a new life."

No, flesh and blood cannot inherit God's kingdom, but thanks to Jesus, who died for us, we've become born again as new creations in Christ (1 Pet 1:3, 23). In the resurrection, we'll be raised up with incorruptible bodies, born of and fueled by the Spirit, which gives life—no longer infected with sin, which leads to death. These new bodies will bear "the image" of the heavenly man—the only man to go to heaven, Jesus Christ.

Rather than prove that believers get a spirit body and live in heaven, this verse in Corinthians supports the consistent Bible truth that we partake of the divine nature now, and when we believe, we are ushered into the kingdom—become subjects of Christ's rule and authority as well as joint heirs, sons and daughters.

CHAPTER 8

"At Home with the Lord" and "Those under the Altar"

HERE WE SEE PAUL again using poetic or figurative language about the hope he held to be united with Christ. While translations break the epistles and gospels into chapters, that's not how these "books" of the Bible were originally written. So let's consider what Paul was talking about in chapter 4 of 2 Corinthians. In that chapter he explains that God, who raised Jesus, will also raise believers, and we should keep our eyes on things that are eternal.

From there he continues, "For we know that if our earthly house, this tent, is destroyed, we have a building from God, a house not made with hands, eternal in the heavens. For in this we groan, earnestly desiring to be clothed with our habitation which is *from* heaven" (2 Cor 5:1–2 NKJV, italics mine). The metaphor continues, describing how we groan (or sigh) because we want to be "further clothed, that mortality may be swallowed up by life" (verse 4).

Take a look at the apostle Peter's similar reference, indicating this wasn't a wholly unusual way to think of one's physical body back in their time: "I think it is right to refresh your memory as long as I live in the tent [Greek: *skenoma*: dwelling place, tabernacle] of this body, because I know that I will soon put it aside, as our Lord Jesus Christ has made clear to me" (2 Pet 1:14–15 NIV).

So here we have the contrast between an earthly tent (which to me aptly pictures our "temporary" housing in this sinful, dying flesh) and a (solid) building from God. What follows is the contrast between being in "the body" and being "at home with the Lord," the latter being something Paul says "we would rather be."

Because this is such an important passage to get right, we're going to spend time digging into some arguments used to infer these verses support a belief in a heavenly reward.

The argument some scholars make is that the condition of being unclothed and naked (verse 4) signifies a disembodied spirit (or soul—they often mix up those two very different words, as you've been seeing) that is meant to await a final body (that's the "intermediate state" that theologians express in vague terms). Supposedly the "building in heaven" is the final, permanent spirit body the faithful will be given at the resurrection (because, for some reason, they believe instead of "sleeping in Christ," faithful believers have to "exist" consciously somewhere in the meantime, awaiting the promised resurrection of both the righteous and the unrighteous).

If you're confused, that's a good thing. Their reasoning is utterly illogical and unsupported by Scripture. To me, it goes against the nature of God, who is a God of order, not confusion! (1 Cor 14:33).

Christian apologist and pastor Robert A. Morey puts it this way in his book *Death and the Afterlife*:

> In [2 Cor 4:16], Paul described man in a dualistic sense of being composed of a perishable body (outer man) and a transcendent soul (inner man) which goes on after death. . . . In 5:1 . . . Death is described as the leaving of the soul to dwell in another place. . . .
>
> Where in Scripture are we told that our resurrection body is already created and waiting in heaven for us? The only rational answer is that Paul is speaking of the soul's dwelling in heaven. . . . The place of dwelling [of the soul] while [the person is] alive is on earth, while the place of dwelling after death is in heaven.[1]

Excuse me, can you repeat that? Only rational answer? What about the only *scriptural* answer?

In 2 Corinthians 4:16, Paul earlier said that Jesus would bring us into his presence, and his statements in other letters support this to mean his return or *parousia* (appearing—see Rom 8:22–25; Phil 3:20–21). Does this mean he hoped, at the resurrection, to be raised from the dead and given a heavenly body?

What helps to understand this passage is that Paul isn't describing the kind of body believers will get but is rather contrasting two states of existence. There is the heavenly "clothing" or building and the earthly tent that is destroyed. The key to getting this passage is this: putting on or being

---

1. Morey, *Death and the Afterlife*, 210.

"At Home with the Lord" and "Those under the Altar"

clothed with a heavenly dwelling is also spoken of as putting on Christ. Romans 13:14 (ESV) says, "But put on the Lord Jesus Christ, and make no provision for the flesh." Notice also Galatians 3:37 (NIV): "For all of you who were baptized into Christ have clothed yourselves with Christ."

It makes more sense that being clothed with our heavenly "dwelling"—in light of other Scriptures and being consistent with all Bible teaching—is talking about Christ's salvation. The Benson Commentary says this about Romans 13:14:

> A strong and beautiful expression for the most intimate union with him, and the being clothed with all the graces which were in him; including the receiving, in faith and love, every part of his doctrine; obeying his precepts, imitating his example, and adorning ourselves therewith as with a splendid robe, not to be put off; because it is the garb intended for that eternal day.[2]

And Matthew Henry says, "The Lord Jesus Christ must be put on as Lord to rule you as Jesus to save you; and in both, as Christ anointed and appointed by the Father to this ruling, saving work."[3]

One more puzzle piece that makes this fit is Jesus's remark at Mark 14:58 (ESV): "I will destroy this temple that is made with hands, and in three days I will build another, not made with hands." Jesus was speaking of his body as a building. This is the same phrase—"not made with hands"—that Paul speaks of regarding the heavenly dwelling. A body that, at baptism, accepts "Christ's clothing" or new life that, at Jesus's return (appearing, coming) will be changed from mortality to immortality in the resurrection.

Since Adam realized he was naked in the garden of Eden once he sinned, it stands to reason Paul's reference to being "naked" is about being in *a sinful state*, and that his mortal body (that dies) will be changed into an immortal one and put on incorruption. Not that his immortal soul will be stripped from his body (hence would now be naked—I have a hard time envisioning naked incorporeal souls floating around in heaven).

Peter speaks of our inheritance, which can never perish, spoil, or fade, being kept in heaven, where it will remain *until* "the coming of the salvation that is ready to be revealed in *the last time*" (1 Pet 1:4–5, italics mine). When you use the word *until*, it means that, at a certain point in time, something is no longer is true. For example: I will stay here *until* I go to

---

2. Benson, *Commentary*, "Romans 13," section Romans 13:14.
3. Henry, *Commentary*, "Romans 13," section Romans 13:11.

the market. Once I leave for the market, I am no longer at my house. Our inheritance—that promised immortal, incorruptible body—is kept safe in heaven *until* Jesus returns—until the "last time." What's the "last time"? It's "the coming of salvation," Jesus's return, which will not show or appear or be revealed until the fixed day and time God set (Acts 17:31).

If we keep in mind that Paul writes in 1 Thessalonians 4:16 that this "putting on of immortality" occurs not at our death but when Jesus returns with a trumpet call, raising first those in Christ (the first resurrection) and, then after, those will be with Christ forever (verse 17), we can be confident Paul is talking about being transformed into a glorious body here on earth. The promises are *kept* in heaven, where they can't rot or be ravaged by the enemy, but the bodies we will be given are incorruptible ones for living on earth. When Jesus returns, he will grab that inheritance that's been stowed away in a "vault," where he's kept it safe, and bestow it upon the faithful when he raises them from the dust of the ground to everlasting life.

Try to look at it another way. Galatians 2:20 says that when we are crucified with Christ, it's not we who live in our bodies any longer but Christ lives in us. When we live in the flesh (without Christ in us), *we are absent from the Lord.*

An article on the website Follow in Truth puts it succinctly:

> Paul then states that all are trying to be accepted of God whether we are present or absent, those that have Christ or those that have not Christ but try (in vain through the law). For everyone must stand before the judgment seat of Christ [2 Cor 5:9 referenced]....
>
> Far from saying that to die is to be with the Lord in heaven—in actual fact when Paul states that he would rather be absent from the body and to be present with Christ he simply means that *he would rather not live in the flesh, living without God but rather to die to self and so live in the spirit that resides in him and therefore be present with the Lord.* [Italics mine.]
>
> 2 Corinthians 5:8 in context has absolutely nothing to do with going to heaven once a believer dies but is actually referring to God dwelling in believers.[4]

We can be present with the Lord now by putting on Christ Jesus, by being born again of the spirit so that Christ lives in us and our lives are hidden in him (Col 3:2–4). And, by remaining faithful, one day we will be resurrected on earth with an incorruptible body that will last forever.

---

4. Thriepland, "2 Corinthians 5:8," paras. 29–31.

"At Home with the Lord" and "Those under the Altar"

Those under the Altar

This final "controversial" Scripture in Revelation 6:9–10 should be prefaced with a reminder that probably isn't needed: the book of Revelation, a vision from Jesus and given to the apostle John, is highly symbolic. It's not literal teaching Jesus gave John; it's a vision, and John describes what he sees and hears in it—including a beast from the sea and a dragon with seven heads and ten horns.

Here's how this passage in chapter 6 reads in the King James Version:

> When he opened the fifth seal, I saw under the altar the souls of those who had been slain for the word of God and the witness they had borne; they cried out with a loud voice, "O Sovereign Lord, holy and true, how long before thou wilt judge and avenge our blood on those who dwell upon the earth?" Then they each were given a white robe and told to rest a little longer, until the number of their fellow servants and their brethren should be complete, who were to be killed as they themselves had been.

Some theologians use this passage as proof positive of faithful believers existing now as souls in heaven awaiting a time when they can be put into some other body. Is it logical to believe all the thousands (millions?) of believers who died for Christ fit in a space under an altar? Well, maybe if it were a big enough altar.

Just as Abel's blood was figuratively crying out from the ground (Gen 4:10), these "souls" (Greek: *psychas*) represent all those martyred for Jesus clamoring to be avenged (see Rev 17:6). In 2 Thessalonians 1:7–8, Paul promises when Jesus returns in flaming fire, it will be to take vengeance on those who did not know and obey Christ—for it is "a righteous thing with God to repay with tribulation those who trouble you" (verse 6).

The blood of animal sacrifices was poured out at the base of the altar, under the Law (Lev 4:7), so because these faithful ones died in sacrifice to their faith, it makes sense these "souls" (their blood) would be positioned here.

So many Bible commentaries get this passage wrong. Take this one, from Biblestudytools.com:

> Though their [referring to the souls under the altar] physical life was terminated, they themselves are still very much alive. Their slaying, then, is not the end of them. It is not the total interruption of their being in all respects. It makes them invisible to men in the

flesh, in the natural state; but it does not hinder their living on as souls, or their being visible to heavenly eyes, or to the eyes of John in his supernatural and prophetic exaltation.... It is altogether a wrong interpretation of the Scriptures which represents the dead in a state of non-existence, unconsciousness, or oblivion.[5]

What's a wrong interpretation of the Scriptures is to teach a doctrine that goes completely contrary to the whole of Scripture. To take one passage and use it to negate everything taught in both the OT and NT is to dismiss the truth of God's Word.

The Bible teaches that when you die, you are dead. You do not come to life until Jesus returns—his appearing—which is a fixed "day" in the future. We have learned that souls die and stay dead until the resurrection. Souls do not live in heaven, not even under an altar.

Yes, this "supernatural and prophetic exaltation" of John's is a symbolic vision. The writer of Hebrews (11:39) says that all those faithful who had died were not made perfect yet but would have to wait until they would be made perfect "together with us."

The image John sees is consistent with those words, as those martyred are told to "rest" until the full number of "brethren" throughout history have been martyred. Yet, the Bible throughout teaches all in Christ are asleep and are waiting to hear Jesus's words so they can "come out of the grave."

Revelation 20:4–5 (NASB) says "And I saw the souls of those who had been beheaded because of their testimony of Jesus and because of the word of God, and those who had not worshiped the beast or his image, and had not received the mark on their forehead and on their hand; and *they came to life* and reigned with Christ for a thousand years" (italics mine). Those souls (individuals, people) under the altar come to life when the chosen faithful sit on those thrones we looked at earlier. Which means that up until this moment (including when they were "crying out" under the altar and then told to rest) they are dead.

It takes a lot of mental wrangling and convoluted arguments to try to justify belief in this passage as literal and supporting the doctrine that those who die in Christ immediately leave their dead bodies behind, become disembodied (naked?) souls, cram under an altar (millions of them?), and are given robes and told to rest (go back to sleep?) until a later time.

---

5. Bible Study Tools, "Revelation 6:9," paras. 5–6.

"At Home with the Lord" and "Those under the Altar"

If you need more scriptural insight on this, jump ahead to the chapter on "Sleeping in Death." Blood cannot talk. Neither can the dead. So, keeping all this in proper context, this vision John saw was symbolic, representing all those who had died in Christ still "waiting," during the Great Tribulation, for that future day of victory and reward.

The Day of God's Wrath

One last passage that, while not using hades or gehenna, is often used to prove that the New Testament supports some belief in hellfire is Romans 2:5–9. The apostle Paul warns of "the day of wrath when God's righteous judgment will be revealed. For he will render to every man according to his works: . . . to those who do not obey the truth, but obey wickedness, there will be wrath and fury. There will be tribulation and distress for every human being who does evil, the Jew first and also the Greek" (ESV).

Again, the best way to understand a passage, aside from seeing other usages of the same words by the same writer, is to reference other Bible writers who use similar language. Often New Testament writers reference the Old Testament, and surely Paul is doing this here. For, take a look at Zephaniah 1:14–15, 18 (NKJV) and pay attention to the fact that the prophet is speaking of the Day of the Lord—Christ's return—not the fate of anyone "wicked" being punished the moment they die:

> The great day of the Lord is near;
> It is near and hastens quickly.
> The noise of the day of the Lord is bitter;
> There the mighty men shall cry out.
> That day is a day of wrath,
> A day of trouble and distress,
> A day of devastation and desolation,
> A day of darkness and gloominess,
> A day of clouds and thick darkness . . . .
> Neither their silver nor their gold
> Shall be able to deliver them
> In the day of the Lord's wrath;
> But the whole land shall be devoured
> By the fire of His jealousy,
> For He will make speedy riddance
> Of all those who dwell in the land.

Isn't Paul alluding to eternal torment when he says these "mighty men" will cry out? Wrath and distress sounds like misery, right? The King James Version makes it sound even worse: "In the fire of his jealous wrath, all the earth shall be consumed; for a full, yea, sudden end he will make of all the inhabitants of the earth."

Yet, since we know immortality is a gift given in the future to the faithful, those whose "souls [lives] will be saved" (Heb 10:39), the wicked will be met with "speedy riddance" or a "sudden end." I don't know if you can twist those phrases to imply eternal torment, but I can't. When we say "good riddance" or "he's come to a sudden end," that's full stop. The person/soul is gone, dead.

Yes, while God is executing his angry judgment against the nations, there will be a lot of pain, suffering, and fear. Just read the whole book of Revelation—you can't miss it. But after all that weeping and gnashing of teeth (see Zeph 1:4; Psalm 112:10 KJV), there comes an end—an end of the lives of those who refuse to accept Jesus as their savior.

CHAPTER 9

Jesus's Use of Gehenna

ANOTHER GREEK WORD TRANSLATED as hell or hellfire is *gehenna*, which can be found in eight passages in the New Testament. We've already looked at the context for verses using hades to show the Bible is wholly consistent from start to finish. Hades is the equivalent of sheol—the nonexistent state of the dead. But some claim Jesus's use of gehenna blows all that out of the water.

Australian theologian Leon Morris reflects that adamant belief:

> Why does anyone believe in hell in these enlightened days? Because Jesus plainly taught its existence. He spoke more often about hell than he did about heaven. We cannot get around this fact. We can understand that there are those who do not like the idea of hell. I do not like it myself. But if we are serious in our understanding of Jesus as the incarnate Son of God, we must reckon with the fact that he said plainly that some people will spend eternity in hell.[1]

I need to point out that since hell will be thrown into the lake of fire, his last sentence doesn't make any sense. Would those unfortunate "souls" be in hell within the lake? Address forwarded? And, no, Jesus didn't talk more about hell than heaven. Sheesh. But let's back up.

Out of the eight times gehenna is used in the New Testament, Jesus uses it seven times (the other instance is found in James 3:6, used in a figurative manner). And, to be more specific, Jesus uses the words always to Jews—not to Gentiles—and in particular to Jews around Jerusalem, who would know what he was referencing.

---

1. Morris, "Dreadful Harvest," lines 1–7.

While there is no argument that "hell" is where the wicked go when they die (though you have learned by now that it's where everyone, including animals and every other physical soul, goes), some feel strongly that Jesus was seemingly sharing a new insight into God's new secret plan to torture individuals. Before we get too carried away, let's remember these verses must be consistent with all of Scripture and reflect God's character.

Where does the word *gehenna* come from, and what did it mean in Jesus's day? This is where context is critical. Jesus spoke to his listeners with the knowledge that they would understand his reference to gehenna—how it was understood in his day.

The transliteration of gehenna is "the Valley of Hinnom," which in ancient days before Christ was a place where the detestable practice of child sacrifice was carried on. This practice entailed burning children alive as an offering to the god Molech (2 Kgs 16:3; 23:10). This was also where the 185,000 bodies of the Assyrians were burned in a massive pyre after God struck them down during Hezekiah's reign, which the Jews of Jesus's day would be familiar with (Isa 30:31–33; 37:36).

As a final confirmation of linking this accursed valley with divine punishment, Jeremiah wrote about Hinnom this way:

> Behold, the days are coming, says the Lord, when it will no more be called Topheth, or the valley of Hinnom, but the valley of Slaughter: for they will bury in Topheth, because there is no room elsewhere. And the dead bodies of this people will be food for the beasts of the air, and for the beasts of the earth; and none will frighten them away. (Jer 7:32–33 ESV; cf. Isa 66:24, where it foreshadows Armageddon in similar imagery)

This is also where the bodies of the slaughtered Jews were dumped after the Roman attack on Jerusalem in 70 AD.[2] So it stands to reason that in the psyche of the first-century Jews, gehenna, or the Valley of Hinnom, would be linked to the thought of a very unpleasant fate. But not at all eternal torture.

A biblical scholar in the nineteenth century, J. W. Hanson, wrote this about Gehenna:

> The Apocrypha, B.C.150–500, Philo Judaeus A.D. 40, and Josephus, A.D. 70–100, all refer to future punishment, but none of them use Gehenna to describe it, which they would have done, being Jews, had the word been then in use with that meaning. Were

2. "Titus' Siege," para. 16.

Jesus's Use of Gehenna

it the name of a place of future torment then, can any one doubt that it would be found repeatedly in their writings? And does not the fact that it is never found in their writings demonstrate that it had no such use then, and if so, does it not follow that Christ used it in no such sense? . . .

Canon Farrar says of Gehenna (Preface to "Eternal Hope"): . . . Used according to Jewish tradition, as the common sewerage of the city, the corpses of the worst criminals were flung into it unburied, and fires were lit to purify the contaminated air. It then became a word which secondarily implied (1) the severest judgment which a Jewish court could pass upon a criminal—the casting forth of his unburied corpse amid the fires and worms of this polluted valley; and (2) a punishment—which to the Jews as a body never meant an endless punishment beyond the grave. Whatever may be the meaning of the entire passages in which the word occurs, "Hell" must be a complete mistranslation, since it attributes to the term used by Christ a sense entirely different from that in which it was understood by our Lord's hearers, and therefore entirely different from the sense in which he could have used it.[3]

It's only later that translations and theologians began to equate the garbage dump of the Gehenna known in Jesus's time with the Hellenistic views of eternal fiery torment. Context is so important here.

Let's now go through these seven passages in which Jesus mentions gehenna. The first three uses of the word are in Matthew chapter 5 (the Sermon on the Mount speech). I've italicized the word used in place of Gehenna (using the New King James Version):

Matthew 5:22, 29–30:

"But I say to you that whoever is angry with his brother without a cause shall be in danger of the judgment. And whoever says to his brother, 'Raca!' shall be in danger of the council. But whoever says, 'You fool!' shall be in danger of *hell fire*. . . . But I say to you that whoever is angry with his brother without a cause shall be in danger of the judgment. And whoever says to his brother, 'Raca!' shall be in danger of the council. But whoever says, 'You fool!' shall be in danger of *hell fire*. "And if your right hand causes you to sin, cut it off and cast it from you; for it is more profitable for you that one of your members perish, than for your whole body to be cast into *hell*."

---

3. Hanson, *Bible Threatenings*, 190–91.

The next four mentions are also in Matthew's gospel:

> Matthew 10:28: "And do not fear those who kill the body but cannot kill the soul. But rather fear him who is able to destroy both soul and body in *hell*."

> Matthew 18:9: "And if your eye causes you to sin, pluck it out and cast it from you. It is better for you to enter into life with one eye, rather than having two eyes, to be cast into *hell fire*."

> Matthew 23:15: "Woe to you, scribes and Pharisees, hypocrites! For you travel land and sea to win one proselyte, and when he is won, you make him twice as much a son of *hell* as yourselves."

> Matthew 23:33: "Serpents, brood of vipers! How can you escape the condemnation of *hell*?"

In Mark, Jesus uses gehenna three times, and it will be helpful to read the surrounding verses:

> Mark 9:43: "If your hand causes you to sin, cut it off. It is better for you to enter into life maimed, rather than having two hands, to go to *hell*, into the fire that shall never be quenched where 'Their worm does not die And the fire is not quenched.'"

> Mark 9:45: "And if your foot causes you to sin, cut it off. It is better for you to enter life lame, rather than having two feet, to be cast into *hell*, into the fire that shall never be quenched where 'Their worm does not die And the fire is not quenched.'"

> Mark 9:47: "And if your eye causes you to sin, pluck it out. It is better for you to enter the kingdom of God with one eye, rather than having two eyes, to be cast into *hell fire*."

Let's start stripping away the assumptions, shall we?

First off, there is no mention in any of these verses of torment. The fire is said to be eternal or not quenched, a place where worms don't die (seemingly fire impervious).

Second, Jesus consistently uses the phrase "throw away" (Greek: *ballo*), "a verb," says scholar Edward Fudge, "that emphasizes the sense of being rejected, banished, and expelled.... This verb, 'to throw away,' has no inherent eschatological significance, but Matthew uses it often when speaking of the doom of the wicked.... Those who go [to gehenna] have been discarded and expelled by God."[4]

---

4. Fudge, *The Fire That Consumes*, 122.

Third, Jesus equates the word *kill* with *destroy*—and it's clear that throughout Scripture these words plainly mean death and nothing more.

Fourth, fire is consistently used to symbolize complete and utter destruction—an apt symbol. Fire utterly destroys things so that they can't be brought back into existence. All that's left, if anything, is ash. That's why the lake of fire—which means the second death—is the "final resting place" of death and hell, as well as of the symbolic "wild beast," the "false prophet," the devil, and his demons. Death is destroyed by Christ—not tortured eternally—and it is thus shown symbolically by being tossed into the lake of fire.

Eternal Judgment

One of the best keys to the biblical symbol of fire is found in Jude 7, in which Jude speaks of the judgment against Sodom and Gomorrah (cities that were destroyed by fire and brimstone), saying they "serve as an example by undergoing a punishment of eternal fire" (ESV, NASB). The NKJV uses the phrase "suffering the vengeance of eternal fire." We see a similar reference in 2 Peter 2:6, where Sodom is spoken of as having been reduced to ashes as an example of what will happen to the wicked.

Are those two cities still burning? Can you go to the Middle East, to Sodom and Gomorrah, and stand on a hill and watch them continue to burn?

Of course not. Yet, the Bible says they are suffering the punishment of eternal fire.

It's the *judgment*—the punishment—that is eternal.

Yet . . . Jesus said those who lived in those cities will not only be resurrected but will "fare better" in the judgment than some of those listening to Jesus when he walked the earth.

If you believe the inhabitants of those cities are burning forever in some hellfire (that somehow the fire of Sodom equates to the fires of "hell"), you are mistaken. Those cities burned and were never rebuilt—not ever in the last roughly four thousand years. It's easy math: eternal judgment and punishment by fire equals utter destruction of those cities.

Take a look at Isaiah 34:9–10 (KJV): "The streams of Edom shall be turned into pitch, and her soil into brimstone; her land shall become burning pitch. Night and day it shall not be quenched, its smoke shall go up for ever."

Is this fire eternal? All we need do is look at the rest of verse 10: "From generation to generation it shall *lie waste;* none shall pass through it for ever and ever" (italics mine).

Is Edom burning today, with streams of pitch? No.

The same expression is made in reference to Babylon the Great in Revelation, which is prophesied to "burn with fire" (Rev 18:8) and "the smoke from her goes up for ever and ever." Verse 19 says "In one hour she has been laid waste." Because of this, the city "shall be found no more" (verse 21). Fire burns so thoroughly, you can't find trace of whatever previously existed.

Often the Bible uses elements of fire, sulfur, and/or brimstone to symbolize complete destruction (Job 18:15; Isa 30:33; Ezek 38:22).

This sounds very much like what we read in Revelation 14:10–11 (which likely drew its language from the passage in Isaiah), where it says that anyone who worships the beast

> shall also drink of the wine of the wrath of God, which is poured out full strength into the cup of His indignation. He shall be tormented with fire and brimstone in the presence of the holy angels and in the presence of the Lamb. And the smoke of their torment ascends forever and ever; and they have no rest day or night, who worship the beast and his image, and whoever receives the mark of his name. (NKJV)

This surely seems to imply judgment of the wicked is all about suffering torment, with "no rest day or night." Yet, from what we've looked at throughout Scripture, we know these facts:

- The dead are not conscious.
- There is no such thing as an immortal soul—the only one ever granted immortality up to this moment is Jesus.
- The wages of sin is death, not eternal torment—when you die, you pay the full price for sin.
- Fire in the Bible symbolizes complete destruction.
- The Bible often uses figurative language, and the book of Revelation is highly symbolic.
- The best way to understand what the Bible means in one place is to locate similar language in other biblical passages.

Jesus's Use of Gehenna

A Fiery, Wormy Garbage Dump

Let's return to gehenna now. Isaiah's foreshadowing image in chapter 66 is likely what Jesus was referencing when he spoke about gehenna as a place where the worm doesn't die (gotta love those immortal worms). Here we read about the future judgment (which also, as often is the case in the Bible, had an immediate historical fulfillment—see Isa 37:36):

> "For behold, the Lord will come in fire,
>   and his chariots like the whirlwind,
> to render his anger in fury,
>   and his rebuke with flames of fire.
> For by fire will the Lord enter into judgment,
>   and by his sword, with all flesh;
> and those slain by the Lord shall be many." (verses 15–16 ESV)

After the Lord slays (not tortures) his enemies, he declares, "From new moon to new moon, and from Sabbath to Sabbath, all flesh shall come to worship before me, declares the Lord. And they shall go out and look on the dead bodies of the men who have rebelled against me. For their worm shall not die, their fire shall not be quenched, and they shall be an abhorrence to all flesh" (verses 23–24).

When we understand that the Bible teaches a person *is* a soul and his eternal fate is in God's hands, we aren't to fear other humans, who could merely destroy our bodies (kill us) but have no authority or control over our eternal prospects. As the psalmist (who is quoted by the writer of Hebrews in chapter 13 verse 6) says: "I trust in God, so why should I be afraid? What can mere mortals do to me?" (Ps 56:4). Only God can throw a person in "gehenna"—an apt symbol for eternal destruction.

Good news for those Sodomites. Though their bodies died in the conflagration of fire and brimstone, they'll get a chance to accept Christ as king in the new earth. Their bodies were destroyed but not their "souls" or ultimate life prospects. Of course, if, at the end of the thousand years, when Satan is let out of prison to test humankind, they side with him against God . . . into the lake of fire they go. And this time, their "soul" will be destroyed.

In Jesus's day, there was no more fitting image of being totally discarded and rejected than the garbage dump of gehenna. In this valley used by the Jews, the fires were kept burning, and whatever the flames didn't consume, the worms and maggots devoured. Because of a constant supply of refuse, the worms and maggots never ran out of food. They never died out due to starvation. They had an "eternal" feast of flesh and detritus.

Getting Thrown into Gehenna

Here's another point. Jesus doesn't use the word "destroy" (*apokteino*—to destroy, slay, kill in any way, inflict mortal death) in the parallel verse in Luke 12:5. He says beware of being "thrown" into gehenna. The fact that God will "destroy both the body and soul" in gehenna plainly eliminates any eternal torment. You can't suffer anything if you are destroyed.

Compare this to Jesus's parable of the sheep and the goats in Matthew 25:41–46, where, after Jesus invites the faithful to enter the kingdom, he says to the unfaithful: "Depart from me, you cursed, into eternal fire prepared for the devil and his angels. . . . And they will go away into eternal punishment, but the righteous into eternal life." Again, that lake of fire, the second death, is eternal *punishment*.

Yes, Revelation describes this lake as the place where the devil, the wild beast, and the false prophet will be "tormented day and night," but we know that is merely symbolic because Hebrews 2:14 says the devil will be brought to nothing, destroyed, so he can't be conscious forever in torment.

As always, the best way to truly understand a biblical use of a word is to examine its usage in the *same Bible book* because the writer of that book knows best what he means. That said, look at how the word *torment* is used in Revelation 9:5; 11:10; and 18:7, 10. You'll see that *torment* is interchangeable with *restraint* or a condition of restraint. The devil and the symbolic beast and false prophet will be restrained for and by eternity, never to exist and trouble humanity ever again, as evidenced from the smoke that "rises for ever and ever" (Rev 14:11).

"Eternal" and "Everlasting"

The Bible has various uses of the words eternal (*aionios*) and everlasting (*aidios*), and context determines the meanings. But one particular way these words are used is to describe the lasting effect of something (gone forever) as opposed to an ongoing process (continual, moment-by-moment experience).

Jesus's Use of Gehenna

Though these two words are used 179 times in the NT, they are only used 12 times when dealing with punishment. The Hebrew equivalent is *owlam*, (439 instances).

A student of the Bible will be hard-pressed to find anything in the Hebrew Scriptures that imply some form of eternal or everlasting torment, but there are plenty of verses that talk about eternity.

Not only is God eternal, but all his qualities are also eternal (of course). Some of the things that are eternal are his ways, love, blessing, plans, reign, protection, righteousness, faithfulness... and on and on.

Where we can run into problems is in thinking that *eternal* or *everlasting* is only used to describe a duration of time. Often the Bible uses the words *eternal* and *everlasting* to mean a length of time, an age, or a period or interval. The Greek word *aion* is used to describe present and past ages (that have or will end—Col 1:26; Gal 1:24) and even future ages (Luke 18:30; 1 Cor 10:11). We read of things said to be "everlasting" that are actually destroyed or done away with in future years (indicating that aion can refer to a limited time period), such as Ammon (Zeph 2:9; Jer 49:6), the Aaronic priesthood (Exod 40:15; Heb 7:14–18), the Law of Moses (Lev 24:8; 2 Cor 3:11,13), Egypt and Elam (Jer 25:27; 49:39), Moab (Jer 48:4, 42, 47), and even Solomon's temple, where God said he would reside "forever" (1 Kgs 8:13) but was later destroyed. It may seem strange to us to speak of something lasting forever that, in actuality, doesn't. But this is how we see this concept expressed in many Bible passages.

However, these words, when applied to punishment, are used to imply permanency. We read in Matthew 25:6 how the righteous are rewarded with eternal life and the unrighteous eternal punishment. If we believe the words *eternal* or *everlasting* apply to time passage, we will conclude that, since such a reward will go on without end, the punishment (an affliction of suffering rather than the sentence of death as the punishment) is endless.

Theologist Samuele Bacchiocchi makes these interesting observations about related terminology in the Dead Sea Scrolls:

> The Damascus Document, an important Dead Sea Scroll, describes the end of sinners by comparing their fate to that of the antediluvians who perished in the Flood and of the unfaithful Israelites who fell in the wilderness. God's punishment of sinners leaves "no remnant remaining of them or survivor" (CD 2, 6, 7). They will be "as though they had not been" (CD 2, 20)....

It is noteworthy that the Manual of Discipline describes the punishment of those who follow the Spirit of Perversity . . . as unending punishment which results in total destruction. The text states: "And as for the Visitation of all who walk in this [Spirit of Perversity], it consists of an abundance of blows administered by all the Angels of destruction in the everlasting Pit by the furious wrath of the God of vengeance, of unending dread and shame without end, and of disgrace of destruction by fire of the region of darkness. And all their time from age to age are in most sorrowful chagrin and bitterest misfortune, in calamities of darkness till they are destroyed with none of them surviving or escaping" (1QS 4.11–14.21).

The fact that the "unending dread and shame without end" is not unending but lasts only "till they are destroyed" goes to show that in New Testament times, people used such terms as "unending," "without end," or "eternal," with a different meaning than we do today. For us, "unending" punishment means "without end," and not until the wicked are destroyed. The recognition of this fact is essential for interpreting later the sayings of Jesus about eternal fire and for resolving the apparent contradiction we find in the New Testament between "everlasting punishment" (Matt 25:46) and "everlasting destruction" (2 Thess 1:9). When it comes to the punishment of the wicked, "unending" simply means "until they are destroyed."[5]

Having this perspective from ancient writings supports the biblical truths that the wicked, though they may experience shame and dread for a time, will, at some point, be destroyed forever.

Think about this too. Psalm 139:7–10 describes how God sees everything everywhere. "Where can I go to escape your presence?" David asks. His answer implies "nowhere." God made everything: space, time, light, darkness, heaven, and hell (sheol). There is only one place you could go where God could not see you. Where you would no longer be in his presence. And that is . . . if you are nowhere to be found. In in word: destroyed.

When Jesus warns that the "goats" will go away into eternal *punishment* (Matt 25:46), this is the same eventuality he's talking about in Matthew 7:13–14 when he says the broad road leads to *destruction*. Just as "everlasting redemption" and "everlasting salvation" mean our redemption and salvation will last forever (and not that we are being continually

---

5. Bacchiocchi, *Immortality*, 203–4.

redeemed or saved every second), so too the everlasting punishment of the "goats" will last forever. I don't think it could be any clearer.

As theologian Edward Fudge put it: "Punishment is the penal consequence for breaking the law imposed by a judicial authority. Punishment is not a duration."[6] Remember: Jude spoke of the cities of Sodom and Gomorrah as "suffering the vengeance of eternal fire" (Jude 7 NKJV). It's the sentence of annihilation that is eternal, not the fire.

Unquenchable Fire

The most pervasive metaphor used in the Bible is fire. In both the Old and New Testaments, God is referred to as a "consuming fire" (Deut 4:24; Heb 12:29). Note that the feature emphasized in this expression is not *burning, torturous,* or *painful* but rather *consuming.*

What does it mean when something's consumed? Some of the definitions the Merriam-Webster dictionary gives for *consumed* are "to do away with completely; destroy; use up, devour, perish."[7]

We see also how John the Baptist warned that, when Jesus came, he would "baptize [people] in the Holy Spirit and in fire . . . he will gather his wheat into the barn but the chaff he will burn up [Greek: *katakaio*] with unquenchable fire" (Matt 3:11–12 NKJV). John the Baptist was the prophet foretold by Malachi, who stated, "Surely the day is coming; it will burn like a furnace. All the arrogant and every evildoer will be stubble, and the day that is coming will set them on fire," says the Lord Almighty. "Not a root or a branch will be left to them" (Mal 4:1 NIV). The burning bush Moses saw was not consumed ("burned up"), but the wicked would be reduced to stubble.

Malachi 4:3 notes: "'You shall trample the wicked, For they shall be ashes under the soles of your feet On the day that I do this,' Says the LORD of hosts" (NKJV). Here, too, we see not eternal torment as the result of God's wrath but ashes. What is left of the wicked can be trampled underfoot. There is nothing mentioned about immortal souls being sent to another location to suffer.

Matthew 18 and Mark 9 both refer to that unquenchable or everlasting (Greek: *aionios*) fire. This is the same expression Jeremiah used regarding the Babylonian destruction of Israel, when he said, "My fury shall be

---

6. Fudge, "Lecture—The Fire That Consumes."
7. Merriam-Webster, s.v. "Consume."

poured out upon this place, upon man, and upon beast, and upon the trees of the field, and upon the fruit of the ground, and it shall burn, and shall not be quenched" (Jer 7:20—cf. Amos 5:6). Of course, Jeremiah was there to witness that this "fire" did go out. It was the *judgment* that was unstoppable, unpreventable.

Ezekiel also uses this imagery in chapter 20 in the way he describes God kindling a fire that will not be quenched. The destruction of the nation of Israel was not by literal fire but by invasion and the forced exodus into exile of the survivors to Babylon.

In Hebrews we read that anyone who keeps sinning after knowing the truth about Jesus and God's plan for salvation faces "a fearful expectation of judgment and of raging fire that will consume the enemies of God" (Heb 10:27 NIV). Note, again, the word *consumed*.

I picture a wildfire raging across dry plains and how, because it is unquenchable (no one there to put it out and no rain in the forecast), everything gets burned to ash. The fire does not go out *until everything is destroyed*. That's the power and symbolism of fire.

When something is unquenchable, it cannot be sated. What an apt description of God's wrath and the fate of the wicked. His fire of judgment cannot be stopped or quenched. It will rage until it completely destroys what it is burning, leaving nothing remaining. It burns until it is done. (For more examples of OT usage of "unquenchable fire," see Isa 1:31; 34:10; Jer 4:4; 7:20; 21:12; Ezek 20:47–48.)

Unable to Escape the Judgment of Gehenna

In the last instance in which Jesus uses gehenna (Matt 23:33), he tells his listeners that "this generation" (those listening to him) would not be able to escape the judgment of gehenna, and they would not pass away (Matt 24:34) until all these things occurred (including this fiery wrath). True to his words, when the Romans destroyed the temple in 70 AD and slaughtered the Jews, those who did not flee to the mountains, as he warned, ended up among the heaps of bodies piled up in the Valley of Hinnom. Do I have to say "context is important"?

Big picture: The Jews of Jesus's day would have understood his language regarding their impending doom to be just a repetition in kind of what befell Israel under the Babylonians. The Jews back then were besieged

Jesus's Use of Gehenna

and destroyed with "unquenchable fire," and so too the Romans were destined to come and do likewise after Jesus had left the earth.

To sum up, Jesus's use of gehenna never once suggests a place of torment. The figurative language paralleling Isaiah's words show that the eternal judgment meant a permanent one. That once God destroyed a person's soul (whole life prospects) and not just his physical body, he would never be resurrected back to life.

The concept of endless torment is inconsistent with the whole of Bible teaching, which portrays the dead as unconscious and awaiting resurrection in the "last day," when Jesus returns and calls everyone from their graves—the righteous and the unrighteous. And, worse, it betrays the heart of a God who says he desires none to be *destroyed* but wishes all the attain to repentance (2 Pet 3:9). Those are the only two options God is offering: destruction or salvation (endless life).

Be careful when you read commentaries about these passages, for you will find a lot of assumptions and interpretations but none backed by Scripture in proper context. Keep in mind, too, that nowhere else in the NT will you find gehenna. Neither Paul nor any of the other letter writers—not even John in Revelation—uses the word. There is mention throughout all of Scripture of "fiery *judgment*," but it has nothing to do with some tormenting fire. Jesus in John 15:6 describes himself as a vine and his followers as branches, and any branch that doesn't abide in him is cast out, thrown into the fire, and burned.

It's encouraging to know the Bible has so many puzzle pieces that construct a wholly consistent picture of every doctrine. We don't have to guess at what fire typifies or symbolizes in the Bible. We have dozens of Scriptures that tell us: fire stands for complete destruction, never literal torment or endless torture. The eternal or everlasting torment of destruction is that it lasts forever—once destroyed, always destroyed.

I don't think the Bible can be any clearer about the prospects for the wicked than in Psalm 92:6–7 (NIV): "Senseless people do not know, fools do not understand, that though the wicked spring up like grass and all evildoers flourish, they will be destroyed forever."

CHAPTER 10

Sleeping in Death

CLEARLY, THERE ARE INSTANCES in the Bible where the Hebrew and Greek words for sleep are referencing literal sleep (Gen 28:16; Matt 25:5; Dan 8:18, for example). Though God never sleeps, he watches over humans while they sleep (Ps 121:4–6). Actual sleep is a comforting, natural thing. Psalm 4:8 (ESV) says, "In peace I will both lie down and sleep [Hebrew: *yashen*]; for you alone, O Lord, make me dwell in safety."

We also see a kind of metaphor usage in the OT, with sleep hinting at laziness or distraction or lack of attention. Even we use expressions like "sleeping on the job," which implies an employee is slacking off and not paying attention. The book of Proverbs has many instances of this (Prov 19:15; 20:13; 24:33–34, to cite a few). In 1 Thessalonians 5:6 we read, "Let us not sleep as do others." The context makes obvious whether literal sleep or metaphoric "sleep" is being used.

Remember: context is one of the three C's, and that involves carefully examining passages to understand how a word is being used—because words often have many usages in Scripture—literal, figurative, metaphoric, and symbolic.

Another way the Bible uses *sleep* is as a metaphor for death, such as in the many instances when the Bible speaks of someone dying and going to "sleep with his forefathers" (an expression used more than thirty times in the OT). Daniel 12:2 says: "Multitudes who sleep in the dust of the earth will awake: some to everlasting life, others to shame and everlasting contempt" (NIV).

The Hebrew word is *shakab*—which basically means "to lie down"— and it can be found more than one hundred times in the OT. Note, though, that *shenah*, which means literal sleep, is never once used in that context of meaning death (sleeping with one's forefathers).

Moses is the first person said to "sleep with his fathers" (Deut 31:16). The next who was said to sleep with his fathers was David (2 Sam 7:12), which is confirmed in 1 Kings 2:10: "And David slept with his fathers, and was buried in the city of David" (ESV). Not just holy or "righteous" people end up "sleeping" like this, though. The same fate is spelled out for evil men, such as Jeroboam, Rehoboam, Abijam, and Baasha.

The New Testament Use of "Sleep"

There are three words translated as sleep in the New Testament. The first is *hupnos*, which gives us the word *hypnosis*, *katheudo*, and *koimaomai*. Hupnos occurs six times—three times in the gospels (Matt 1:24; Luke 9:32; John 11:13), twice in Acts (Acts 20:9), and once in Romans 13:11, used in a figurative sense.

Katheudo occurs twenty-one times and refers to ordinary physical sleep or failure to keep watch (figurative "stay awake") rather than the involuntary falling asleep in death (see Eph 5:14; 1 Thess 5:6–7, 10).

Koimaomai is used eighteen times. Katheudo means to sleep (condition of sleep), in contrast with koimaomai, which means to *fall* asleep out of sheer weariness or unto death.

We read in Luke 22:45: "He found them sleeping for sorrow" and in 1 Corinthians 11:30: "For this cause many are weak and sickly among you, and many sleep."

Jesus stated Lazarus was dead, plainly, after he first said he was asleep (koimaomai), having died after being ill (Luke 8:52). Just as Lazarus was asleep (John 11:11), saints are also said to sleep (Matt 27:52). Christ is the first to be resurrected from sleep (1 Cor 15:18), and Stephen also "fell asleep" in death (Acts 7:60).

What's interesting is nowhere in the NT are unbelievers said to be asleep in this way. Jesus never told the rebellious religious leaders, "You will fall asleep [koimaomai] in your sins"; instead, he said they will *die* (*apothneskoi*) in their sins because, without accepting Jesus's sacrifice to cover their sins, they were still under the law, and the sting of the law is the penalty of death (John 8:24)—they would not sleep "in Christ," promised immortality. Apothnesko's usage in the NT means to die, to be no more, to perish, the natural death of man or animal.[1]

This is the reason believers who "die in the Lord" are said to be blessed (Rev 14:13). They may die and "sleep" in the dust for a time, but they are promised a resurrection that precludes them from *ever being destroyed* (in the lake of fire, which symbolizes eternal destruction). Paul says that when Jesus returns, the dead in Christ will rise first (1 Thess 4:16), and in Revelation we read, "Blessed and holy is he who has part in the first resurrection. Over such the second death has no power" (Rev 20:6. See also Rev 2:11–12).

Surely if Paul believed those who died believing in Christ—those sealed for the future day of redemption (Eph 4:30)—immediately went from grave to heaven as bodiless souls, he would have mentioned it, to comfort the families of those dead believers. But he didn't.

The word translated as "will rise" (Greek: *anistemi*) comes from two words that mean to stand again, though the word commonly means resurrection. It is never in the Bible translated as heaven or refers to going to heaven. The dead—as all the other Scriptures in both the Old and New Testaments clearly say of everyone resurrected—will be resurrected on earth, terra firma, this planet. Our home.

In John 11:25–26, Jesus said, "I am the resurrection and the life. Whoever believes in me, though he die, yet shall he live. And everyone who lives and believes in me shall never die" (ESV). You have to actually die first (because the wages of sin is death), as Paul says plainly in his letter to the Romans. But if you believe in Jesus and accept his propitiatory sacrifice to pay your debt, you will not have death as your future. "Though [we] die," Jesus says, we shall "never die [be sentenced to eternal death]."

And because we are not at all conscious when we are dead, it will be as if we are changed from death to life in a twinkling of an eye. Believers in Jesus as God's arm of salvation will be transformed into a perfect "spiritual" human body, one that will not be subject to the risk or fate of the second death (Rev 2:11; 20:6). That is different from those who did not die "in Christ" who will come to life on earth for a period of judgment.

No wonder Paul said in 2 Corinthians 6:2: "For God says, 'At just the right time, I heard you. On the day of salvation, I helped you.' Indeed, the 'right time' is now. Today is the day of salvation" (NLT). There is no better day to accept the pathway to salvation that Jesus offers—made available by his finished work on the cross—than today, right now. Because those who

---

1. Strong, *Concordance*, s.v. "Apothnesko," G599.

are born again of the spirit *in this life* will be raised incorruptible, sealed for eternity, and will never be subject to destruction. It is truly a gift that should make us speechless with gratitude.

All Dogs and People Do Not Go to Heaven

This truth about believers currently sleeping in death is a very hard one for many Christians. They are comforted in believing their loved ones are now "with the Lord," perhaps watching over them from heaven (although, I always thought that was a bit creepy, like voyeurism). They are comforted in believing those loved ones are hanging with Jesus right now, waiting for the day when they themselves will get turned into a spirit and live in heaven—until they get put back on earth in some other body.

David Jeremiah, who is described on his book's Amazon product page as having "spent a lifetime studying what the Bible has to say about heaven," says,

> In the New Testament, the Greek word translated "to fall asleep" is *koimao*, which comes from the same Greek root as "to lie down." *Koimao* was also used to describe someone who slept in a hotel for one night and the next day would get up to continue his or her journey. This is a beautiful image of what happens to believers' bodies when they die. Their bodies go to sleep, awaiting the Resurrection at the Rapture—while their souls and spirits go to be with our Lord in heaven.[2]

I'm sad to see what a lifetime of studying the Bible has led this diligent student to conclude, for that is not what the Bible teaches. Neither our souls (ourselves) nor our spirits (the breath of life that animates our corporeal bodies) fly up to heaven to be with Jesus while our (empty?) bodies are asleep. This isn't a case of "going home to be with the Lord." Rather, on that day of resurrection that Jesus spoke of repeatedly, he will call out, and all the dead will rise from their graves and, at some point, every knee will bend and every tongue will confess that Jesus is Lord to the glory of God the Father (Phil 2:10; also see Rom 14:11). There is a new earth in which righteousness is to dwell (2 Pet 3:13). No, not a new planet. Or some "symbolic earth." When Jesus said the meek will inherit the earth, he meant *this* earth. He was quoting Psalm 37, which repeatedly speaks of how one day

---

2. Jeremiah, *Answers to Your Questions*, 12.

the wicked will be no more on *this* earth. You'll look around for them, but they'll be gone. That's not happened yet, ever, on this planet.

This is what Jesus meant by "one being taken and one left behind" when he returns (Matt 24:40–42). No, the faithful aren't the ones taken (removed, destroyed) or "raptured" to heaven; they are the ones who remain, who inherit the earth. How can we be sure? Well, read verses 37–39 (NKJV):

> "But as the days of Noah were, so also will the coming of the Son of Man be. For as in the days before the flood, they were eating and drinking, marrying and giving in marriage, until the day that Noah entered the ark, and did not know until the flood came and took them all away, so also will the coming of the Son of Man be."

Who is taken back in Noah's day, according to that passage? The unfaithful. They were swept away, drowned. Noah was kept safe. Kept alive here on earth. *Just as in Noah's day . . .* that means it will be the same—wicked people will be destroyed. The righteous will be left, the survivors of God's wrath.

Peter notes that "the earth of old was destroyed" by that great flood. But was the actual planet obliterated? No. What "earth" was "destroyed"? It was human society (Greek: *kosmos*, which in the NT is used for the earth, human society, human affairs, humans alienated from God—more generally used as an order of things). We know by the context in Peter's letter that he's talking about evil humans and how God "knows how to preserve the righteous and destroy the wicked in the day of judgment." His description of the earth being destroyed by fire instead of water this time then cannot (keeping faithful to context and comparison) mean the earth will burn and everyone on it will die.

And, honestly, what would be the point of literally burning the earth if sinful souls were then to be sent to an eternal burning fire for punishment? That's like burning down a bad man's house after arresting him for murder. Why should the house be "punished"? And how does that make sense if the curse upon the earth—the literal earth—is to be removed when Jesus takes the throne (Rev 22:3)? Why announce a removal of the curse from the earth, and leaves of trees provided for the healing of the nations, if you plan to burn the planet to a crisp? You have to put all these pieces together in context in a consistent way and in harmony with God's loving and just character.

As we've seen, fire is used as a symbol of permanent destruction (when it's not used as a metaphor for purification). Jude 7 speaks of Sodom and Gomorrah as serving "as an example by undergoing a punishment of eternal fire." Remember: Sodom is not still burning. Fire rained down and utterly destroyed that city in one day, never to exist again. There are many more verses that support this consistent teaching in the Bible. Anytime the Bible talks about fire symbolically, it means complete destruction. That's why the second death is likened to a lake of fire. Once you are thrown into it, you are destroyed. Period.

All this to say: this earth, full of sin and evil, will burn with "fire"—all of the systems now in place and ruled by Satan will be obliterated. Gone forever. Replaced by "New Jerusalem" coming down from heaven to this "renewed" earth (Rev 21:2).

John's Vision of the Great Crowd

If this is true—that no human other than Jesus ever goes to heaven, how do we fit Revelation chapter 7 into context? Let's take a look at verses 9–17 in the NKJV, in which John describes what he sees after watching 144,000 "servants" from the twelve tribes of Israel get "sealed"—presumably to protect them from the harm about to be meted out on the inhabitants of Earth.

> After these things I looked, and behold, a great multitude which no one could number, of all nations, tribes, peoples, and tongues, standing before the throne and before the Lamb, clothed with white robes, with palm branches in their hands, and crying out with a loud voice, saying, "Salvation belongs to our God who sits on the throne, and to the Lamb!" All the angels stood around the throne and the elders and the four living creatures, and fell on their faces before the throne and worshiped God, saying:
>
> "Amen! Blessing and glory and wisdom,
> Thanksgiving and honor and power and might,
> Be to our God forever and ever. Amen."
>
> Then one of the elders answered, saying to me, "Who are these arrayed in white robes, and where did they come from?"
> And I said to him, "Sir, you know."
> So he said to me, "These are the ones who come out of the great tribulation, and washed their robes and made them white in the blood of the Lamb. Therefore they are before the throne of

God, and serve him day and night in His temple. And He who sits on the throne will dwell among them. They shall neither hunger anymore nor thirst anymore; the sun shall not strike them, nor any heat; for the Lamb who is in the midst of the throne will shepherd them and lead them to living fountains of waters. And God will wipe away every tear from their eyes."

God's throne is in heaven—Scriptures are clear about that. And Jesus, in heaven, has a throne alongside his Father's. Here we see this uncountable crowd of faithful ones who come out of the Great Tribulation on earth, saved and redeemed—as evidenced by their robes made white or pure by means of Jesus's shed blood. Yet, they are shown to be in heaven, similar to those we saw "under the altar." The verses state that they are right in front of that heavenly throne, serving him day and night in his temple.

To all appearances, these humans have been given some "spiritual" body and now, forever, reside in heaven. But let's deconstruct this.

We read how God will dwell among them (verse 15), and they will hunger and thirst no more. God will wipe away every tear from their eyes. Where else do we find these words in the New Testament, and what is the context there? This very image and much of the same wording is found in Revelation 21, so let's compare—using the rule of the three C's—for the best way to understand a Bible passage is to examine how the same words, phrases, and concepts are used in other parts of the Bible. And especially when used in the same Bible book written by the same author.

> I, John, saw the holy city, New Jerusalem, coming down out of heaven from God, prepared as a bride adorned for her husband. And I heard a loud voice from heaven saying, "Behold, the tabernacle of God is with men, and He will dwell with them, and they shall be His people. God himself will be with them and be their God. And God will wipe away every tear from their eyes; there shall be no more death, nor sorrow, nor crying. There shall be no more pain, for the former things have passed away." (Rev 21:2-4 NKJV)

What do we notice here? God himself will dwell with mankind, that his tabernacle or temple is *with men*. The Greek word for dwell—*skenoo*—means to fix one's tent, occupy, or encamp. The holy city, where God's throne resides (because that's where God resides), now comes down *out of heaven* to encamp among humans. It's interesting that of the five times this Greek word is used in the NT, four times are found in Revelation, and the fifth describes Jesus as temporarily dwelling "among us" when he came to earth via birth as a human (the first instance of his appearing, in order to save us—John 1:14).

Think about that a moment. If something is coming *down* from heaven, it is no longer *in* heaven.

These holy ones in white robes are said to be before the throne day and night, as well as the angels and crowned "twenty-four elders," who also have thrones and reign alongside Christ (Rev 4:4—symbolic of some unidentified group of faithful humans, since angels are never shown given or wearing crowns or sitting on thrones, whereas humans are clearly foretold to rule with Christ). While this is a picture of a heavenly scene, showing heavenly and earthly beings all in accord in worship, we're again reminded that the kingdom descends to earth, and that's where death will be no more (since there isn't any death in heaven to eradicate), and where God will wipe away tears and where the faithful will drink from the "fountain of the water of life freely" (Rev 21:6).

John's vision, full of symbolism, is showing this great crowd of faithful before God's throne and the assembly of heaven as a way of representing them approved and saved and grateful. But does this literally mean they are in heaven itself?

We, individually in prayer, can approach the throne of grace and enter into God's presence now (Heb 4:16). We aren't literally taken into the heavenly realm when we pray.

Ephesians 2:4–6 points out that we are already sitting on thrones with Christ—now, while we are alive here on earth in this broken world:

> But God, being rich in mercy, because of the great love with which he loved us, even when we were dead in our trespasses, made us alive together with Christ—by grace you have been saved—and raised us up with him and seated us with him in the heavenly places in Christ Jesus. (ESV)

Right now, neither you nor I are literally sitting in heaven with Christ. But *positionally*, in God's eyes, we are there, in a place of honor, adopted into his family. We can enter with boldness into God's presence because of Jesus's death on the cross which rent the heavy curtain of the heavenly temple that separated us and prevented access (Heb 10:20–22). We can stand before his throne, day and night, praising and worshipping him without leaving our homes. Right now, in this very moment, our lives are hidden with Christ in God (Col 3:2–4). Colossians 1:22 says, "Yet now he has reconciled you to himself through the death of Christ in his physical body. As a result, he has brought you *into his own presence*, and you are holy and blameless as you *stand before him* without a single fault" (NLT, italics mine). This occurs now, not in some future time, when "souls" or "spirits" are resurrected to heaven.

Christ is in heaven, yet he is also "in us" (Col 1:27). This isn't a physical paradox. This is a picture of spiritual union that transcends time and space.

These passages in Revelation tell how God will, again—as he did with Adam in the garden—dwell or commune with humans on earth.

Back in Adam's day, God still "resided" in heaven—he always has and always will because the heavens belong to God, but the earth he has given to the sons of men (Ps 115:16). Heaven is God's throne; the earth is his footstool (Isa 66:1). He visited Adam in the "cool of the day" (Gen 3:8 NIV) without relinquishing his permanent dwelling place in heaven.

It's hard to wrap our minds around our Creator's existing outside of time and space, and we need to remind ourselves that heaven isn't merely the sky above or some material "place" in this created universe. God, before creating anything, existed. Forever, outside of time and eternity. And that "place" where God exists in that inexplicable dimension is "heaven." Angels are in some part of the heavenly realm—a created spirit realm—but we don't have a clue if they have access to the "heavens of the heavens" God resides in outside of time and space. Angels, being created, seem to live inside of time. I'm not trying to confuse you, but we need to realize how much we *don't* know about heaven and "heavenly realms."

But this we do know—this earth is our forever home. It will be turned into the paradise God promised and intended from the start. God's word will not fail or return void to him. He will see it through—humanity dwelling "with God" here on earth in fellowship, the way he started out with Adam. He never made Adam to be of heaven. While the "tent of God" will reside once more with mankind, with God "dwelling among them," just as he "dwelled" in fellowship with Adam and Eve, God's presence will be with us. But God *resides* in heaven—that's his permanent address. He visited the Tent of Meeting—the portable sanctuary—in the wilderness with Moses (Exod 33:7–11). He filled the temple Solomon built but didn't actually reside there, and that wise king noted in 2 Chronicles 2:6: "But who is able to build him a house, since heaven, even highest heaven, cannot contain him? Who am I to build a house for him, except as a place to make offerings before him?" (ESV).

Yes, God will always reside in heaven—heaven belongs to God. But the earth he's given to humankind. We have been made to live on earth; it is our inheritance.

CHAPTER 11

Meeting the Lord in the Air

I WANT TO GO deep into something here. For years it confused me that Paul seemed to imply he believed he would still be alive when Christ returned. Why would he believe such false information? Surely if he proclaimed this as truth and it was included in the Bible, then it had to be true. Which meant that Jesus came back sometime in the first century, resurrected all the faithful, who met "the Lord in the air" to be with him for eternity.

The passage in question here is 1 Thessalonians 4:16–17. Let's read it in the New King James Version:

> For the Lord Himself will descend from heaven with a shout, with the voice of an archangel, and with the trumpet of God. And the dead in Christ will rise first. Then we who are alive and remain shall be caught up together with them in the clouds to meet the Lord in the air. And thus we shall always be with the Lord.

But notice what he says in 1 Thessalonians 4:15, the prior verse: "For this we say to you by the word of the Lord, that we who are alive and remain until the coming of the Lord will by no means precede those who are asleep."

There's that word again: asleep. Paul says he isn't going to be raised up *before* (precede) those who are asleep (dead) in Christ. Since the Bible repeatedly speaks of a specific day (which could be some length of time—a time period) when both the righteous and unrighteous will hear Jesus's voice and come out of their graves, he must be referring to that future day, which has not come yet.

In Luke 20:38, Jesus says, in referencing Abraham, Isaac, and Jacob (who clearly were still dead in the first century), "For He is not the God of the dead but of the living, for all live to him" (or "They are all alive to him"—NLT; cf. Mark 12:27).

I love how the Bible is a puzzle, with every piece helping show where other pieces go. Jesus states that those dead—the faithful who are asleep—are *alive to God, right now*. Whether Paul meant he would be alive *to God* at that future time, or he is using "we" (who are alive and remain) to mean members of the faith in the future, at that moment when Jesus returns, I don't know. There are plenty of interpretations about this. But one thing the Bible is consistent on: the reward is here on earth. Jesus's kingdom comes down from heaven—"Behold, the dwelling place of God is with man. He will dwell with *them* [not "they will go reside with him"] and they will be his people" (Rev 21:3 ESV, italics mine)—and the meek will inherit the earth (Matt 5:5). Jesus said God has many rooms in his father's abode (John 14:2) and was going to prepare a place for his believers, but that place is brought to earth, where we will reside.

The one and only verse that implies a "rapture" is where Paul in 1 Thessalonians speaks of "being caught up with the Lord in the clouds." In Acts, the angel says that Jesus, after departing into the clouds, will "return the same way" (Acts 1:11). Jesus mentioned many times that he would be coming on "the clouds" when he returned. We are told variations: "coming with the clouds," "coming on the clouds," "coming in the clouds" (Matt 24:30; 26:64; Mark 13:26)— no doubt tying in with the Scripture in 1 Corinthians 10:1–2, in which Paul speaks of the literal cloud the Israelites walked in/within/under when in the wilderness, and that, symbolically, they were baptized into Moses via that cloud.

The word for cloud is used as a symbol of divine presence, something that hides God's glory (Exod 16:10; 33:9; Num 11:25; 12:5; Job 22:14; Ps 18:11). At the dedication of the temple, a cloud "filled the house of the Lord" (1 Kgs 8:10). So it makes sense that when Jesus returns, he'll be encompassed by clouds (glory).

The Greek word for "caught up" (*harpazo*) means to be seized, taken by force, snatched, or claim for oneself eagerly.[1] In John 10:28, the same word is used: "And I give them eternal life, and they shall never perish; neither shall anyone snatch them out of My hand" (NKJV). No one will snatch us but Jesus, to save us for eternity.

The Bible has so many Scriptures about our future here on earth—how God's kingdom will rule here, and the nations will stream to Zion and

---

1. Strong, *Concordance*, s.v. "Harpazo," G726.

learn war no more, and the animals will live in peace, and no one will have to tell his neighbor "know God" because everyone will know him just as the waters cover the seas (Hab 2:14; Isa 11:9. See also Jer 31:34). Isaiah 9:7 promises: "Of the greatness of [Jesus's] government and peace there will be no end. He will reign on David's throne and over his kingdom, establishing and upholding it with justice and righteousness from that time on and forever. The zeal of the Lord Almighty will accomplish this" (NIV). These things have not happened yet!

Remember: Jesus quoted from Psalm 37:11 when he said, "The meek will inherit the earth." The verse in Psalms continues with "and shall delight themselves in the abundance of peace" (that surely hasn't come to pass yet either).

I mentioned this in the previous chapter, how Jesus likened his coming to the days of Noah (Matt 24:38–41), when all humanity was "taken" by a flood and Noah and his family were kept alive, on earth. But let's revisit this to understand Paul's phrase about "meeting the Lord in the air."

> "For in the days before the flood, people were eating and drinking, marrying and giving in marriage, up to the day Noah entered the ark; and they knew nothing about what would happen until the flood came and took them [carry off, move from its place, remove] all away. That is how it will be at the coming of the Son of Man. Two men will be in the field; one will be taken and the other left. Two women will be grinding with a hand mill; one will be taken and the other left." (NIV)

Since Jesus says plainly "This is how it will be"—exactly like in Noah's day—we can presume he means the righteous are the ones who will be left behind (not raptured), and the unsaved will be taken (removed). This is also confirmed by the parable in Matthew 25 about the sheep and the goats. The "sheep" inherit the kingdom prepared for them (the same kingdom that will come down from heaven to earth in Revelation), whereas the "goats" get sent to everlasting punishment (Greek: *kolasis*, used only two times in the NT and mean punishment—cf. 1 John 4:18).

I like how this article on the Crossway Organization website explains it:

> There are difficulties in 1 Thessalonians for the rapture theory. This interpretation would imply that Jesus' glorious descent is only partial, stopping in the clouds/air briefly in order to meet the raptured Christians before returning to heaven with them.

> It seems more likely that Paul expects Jesus' descent to continue from the heavens to the earth. Thus many have argued that the verb for "meet" in the phrase "meet the Lord in the air" is key to understanding these anticipated events.
>
> This Greek word for "meet" (*apantesis*) appears in only two other NT texts. In the eschatological parable of Matthew 25:6, the virgins wait for the bridegroom, whom they "meet" and welcome back to the wedding feast. In Acts 28:15, Roman believers travel out to the Forum of Appius in order to welcome Paul and bring him back to Rome with them. In both Matthew 25 and Acts 28, the action of meeting involves going forth to greet an honored person, then promptly returning with the honored guest.
>
> Many instances of apantesis in the Septuagint Greek OT follow a comparable pattern (e.g., Judg 4:18; 11:31, 34; 19:3; 1 Sam 13:10), and secular Greek writings use the word to speak of civic delegations going out to welcome a dignitary before returning in celebration to the city.
>
> This would imply that, at Christ's appearance, Paul expects the dead in Christ to be raised, followed by the lifting up of the living believers to welcome Jesus in the air, before Jesus descends to earth with his people in order to judge the world and establish fully his kingdom on earth....
>
> Some have suggested that "in the air" metaphorically implies something like "out in the open," perhaps in the midst of the clouds that have descended all the way to earth with Jesus. However, it is more probable that Paul intends the "air" and "clouds" to be used to designate a physical space between the earth and the heavens.[2]

Jesus is coming with the clouds, and "every eye will see him." We don't know exactly how that will play out because, when Jesus appears, he can't be everywhere in the sky over the entire earth at one time. Maybe it will be some kind of psychic broadcast into the minds of the billions of people around the globe, an awareness of his presence (*parousia*) upon his return. I've even heard some speculate that because we now have the internet and social media, that's how every "eye will see him." I doubt, though, that every single person, from the jungles of the Amazon to the impoverished neighborhoods of Bangladesh, has access to the internet. However Jesus pulls this off, we know he has the power, his word is true, and he'll accomplish this. The one who created our brains and eyes can surely find a way for us to see Jesus when he returns with those clouds.

---

2. Crossway, "Rapture," paras. 15–16.

But Jesus's return will trigger the resurrection of those asleep in Christ (dead) first, and then those "alive and remaining" (remaining after what? Possibly those who survive the Great Tribulation) will greet their Lord, who is coming in the air, down from heavens in a cloak of clouds (glory), to welcome him back to earth to rule for a thousand years. On earth. With humans. For "the tent of God is with mankind, and he will be their God and they will be his people."

Remember: Isaiah 55:11 says that when God declares he will do something, it won't fail. It will do exactly what he said he would do. God put humans on the earth to subdue it and be stewards of it. "The highest heavens belong to the Lord, but the earth he has given to mankind" (Ps 116:15 NIV). That word he sent forth has not yet returned with the results he intended. But it will—when Jesus brings all things together under him via his rule and then, after the thousand years are up, he turns the kingdom back over to his father, God (1 Cor 15:24).

It's really quite simple.

Since the whole Bible foretells humans living on earth, where they were designed to live, forever into eternity (see Eccl 1:4), there has to be some reason Paul spoke of some believers being snatched by Jesus when he comes in/on/with the clouds upon his return.

Being Snatched by Jesus

Is it possible that this "snatching" is figurative? The word means forceful, taken by force, seized. That seems an odd word if describing a *literal* action of Jesus. Why would he need to almost violently, forcefully snatch his faithful ones into a cloud (the same word is used with great symbolism in Revelation 12:5 about the male child being snatched up to heaven before it can be harmed)? The verse says those believers will be "caught up with the Lord in the clouds." It doesn't specify that we believers, for example, will be *in* the clouds. But we know, without a doubt, that *Jesus* will be in the clouds (or with, on, surrounded by).

Consider this. Just as we noted with the words of Jesus on the cross, there aren't any commas or other punctuation in the oldest Greek texts. As with Jesus's words to the thief hanging on the cross beside him, we have a similar punctuation situation with this verse: "Then we who are alive and remain shall be caught up together with them [those resurrected from sleeping "in Christ," participants of the "first resurrection"] in the clouds to meet the Lord in the air. And thus we shall always be with the Lord" (NKJV). It doesn't clearly say *we* are going to go into the clouds, into the air, to meet the Lord. It more likely, based on all the supporting Scriptures in the Bible, means it's *the Lord* who is in the air, coming on clouds, coming down to earth. If Jesus comes to earth via the air on/in/with the clouds, we can meet him here on the ground, caught up, snatched, seized, taken by the force of his love and presence to preserve our lives so we can live with him forever.

Remember: one of the meanings of the word is "to claim for oneself eagerly." Of all the usages of harpazo in the NT, this one resonates with me regarding this verse. I can't wait for Jesus to eagerly claim me for himself—to snatch me up in love—so where he is, I can be with him forever, here on earth.

This makes so much more sense to me and is harmonious with all Scripture. If we were to take that verse alone, literally, then we have Jesus violently seizing his followers in a negative, forceful way—which is how the word harpazo is used often in the Bible (thirteen times)—and for some reason hanging out in midair (doing what?). There is nothing dangerous he needs to snatch us from in that moment he returns.

Think about these instances of harpazo. "No man will snatch [my sheep] out of my hand," Jesus says (John 10:28—see also verse 29). The wicked one snatches the seed before it can root in the heart, in the parable at Matthew 13:19. In 2 Corinthians 12:2 and 4, Paul recounts a vision in which he was caught up or snatched up into "third heaven" or some kind of paradise. It's a very odd and vague reference to some other man, though he appears to be speaking of himself. Since it's symbolic, we have to be careful not to misapply the usage of harpazo to reference some rapture of the saints.

The Hour of Trial Afflicting All Those Who Dwell on Earth

The rapture of the saints, while an image that is comforting to believers, is unscriptural. No one wants to suffer during the Great Tribulation, which is described in graphic symbolic detail in the book of Revelation, but if we understand that no one ever goes to heaven, that means believers who are alive during this outpouring of God's wrath will have to go through it.

Jesus assures the church at Philadelphia (which is likely symbolic of a group of believer "types" rather than a literal church in the first century) "that since you have kept my command to endure patiently, I will also keep you from the hour of trial that is going to come on the whole world to test the inhabitants of the earth" (Rev 3:10 NIV). What Jesus means by "keep you" isn't explained (the Greek word here means to take care of or guard), but nowhere does this promise removal from the earth.[3]

Revelation 7:2–3 indicates that those in Christ will be shielded and spared from suffering *some specific* punishments intended for unbelievers (to test their hearts and see if they'll repent): "Then I saw another angel ascending from the rising of the sun, with the seal of the living God, and he called with a loud voice to the four angels who had been given power to harm earth and sea, saying, 'Do not harm the earth or the sea or the trees, until we have sealed the servants of our God on their foreheads'" (ESV). And when the plague of stinging locusts are about to be unleashed upon the earth, we read: "They were told not to harm the grass of the earth or any green plant or any tree, but only those people who do not have the seal of God on their foreheads" (Rev 9:4 ESV).

Instead of all believers alive at the time Christ returns to destroy those who are destroying the earth (Rev 11:18) being whisked up to heaven to watch from a safe distance, numerous passages in this Bible book show that Christians are not only on the earth and going through this distress along with the rest of the world, they suffer. There is a great crowd who, during this time, "wash their robes and [make] them white in the blood of the Lamb" (Rev 7:13–14 NKJV)—meaning, they become believers during this time (because it's God's will that as many as possible repent and turn to him to be saved)—but they are not the only believers on earth at this moment.

Here are some of the verses that indicate that believers—whether newly converted or already born again prior to Christ's return—will not be spared from tribulation:

> "Anyone who is destined for prison will be taken to prison. Anyone destined to die by the sword will die by the sword. This means that God's holy people must endure persecution patiently and remain faithful." (Rev 13:10 NLT; cf. Rev 14:12)

> "Here is a call for the endurance of the saints, those who keep the commandments of God and their faith in Jesus." (Rev 14:12 ESV)

> "Then the dragon became furious with the woman and went off to make war on the rest of her offspring, on those who keep the

---

3. Strong, *Concordance*, s.v. "Tereo," G5083.

commandments of God and hold to the testimony of Jesus." (Rev 12:17 ESV)

"Also [the beast] was allowed to make war on the saints and to conquer them." (Rev 13:7 ESV)

"The second beast was given power to give breath to the image of the first beast, so that the image could speak and cause all who refused to worship the image to be killed." (Rev 13:15 NIV)

"Then I heard a voice from heaven say, 'Write this: Blessed are the dead who die in the Lord from now on.' 'Yes,' says the Spirit, 'they will rest from their labor, for their deeds will follow them.'" (Rev 14:13 NIV)

Note how that last verse aligns with all Bible teaching that states when the dead die, they are "at rest" or sleeping in the grave. But they are blessed because they are not only spared from further pain or suffering, their deeds "follow them." They are rewarded for their faithfulness by being granted a resurrection of the righteous—which comes with the gift of an incorruptible body and immunity from the second death. "Be faithful until death, and I will give you the crown of life," Jesus promises (Rev 2:10 NKJV).

To summarize: those dead "in Christ" are asleep in him. Their lives are hidden in Christ, and we are told, "When Christ, who is your life, is revealed to the whole world, you will share with him in all his glory" (Col 3:4 NLT). They will share in his glory by being raised up to everlasting life in an incorruptible body like Jesus's, when he returns.

The unrighteous will also be resurrected, but to judgment. They will have a thousand years to "get with the program," and at the end of that time period, Satan will be let loose from his prison and will convince a third of humanity to turn against God and side with Satan (Rev 20:7). Those who do will be destroyed in the lake of fire, which "means" the second death—no hope of ever being resurrected (the final section of this book, Judgment, will explain this thoroughly).

This is why Scripture says, "Blessed are those who sleep in Christ—the second death has no power over them." Jesus said to the woman at the well that those who believed in him would have everlasting life welling up inside them, an eternal spring of life—life in themselves (John 4:14). The generating of endless life is a feature of the perfect resurrected body given to the faithful. Truly, that is the great blessing we receive from Christ's sacrifice. All we must do is "believe in the Son of God" and accept this free gift.

"Where I Am Going, You Cannot Follow"

In the book of John, we see a discussion with Jesus and his apostles in which Jesus speaks of going to a place where they cannot follow, but he then says, specifically to Peter, "You can't go with me now, but you will follow me later" (John 13:36 NLT).

Wouldn't that clearly imply Jesus is speaking about heaven? At this Lord's Supper, on Passover evening before Jesus's crucifixion, we see Jesus preparing his close companions for what is soon to transpire. Let's look at the context because—as you should know by now—context is paramount.

Since we already understand from the Hebrew Scriptures and many passages in the New Testament that *no human* has ever gone to heaven, and that Jesus would be the firstfruits of those raised from the dead to eternal life in an immortal body (those whom Elijah, Jesus, Paul, and others raised from the dead went on to die again—they hadn't yet fully paid the wage of sin), this passage has to be consistent with all the rest of Bible teaching.

Acts 26:22-23 records Paul saying: "To this day I have had the help that comes from God, and so I stand here testifying both to small and great, saying nothing but what the prophets and Moses said would come to pass: that the Christ must suffer and that, by being the first to rise from the dead, he would proclaim light both to our people and to the Gentiles" (ESV; see also Rev 1:5). The Bible is consistently clear: no one was resurrected to heaven before Jesus—he is the first. But he is also the last to go to heaven.

After Jesus has washed the disciples' feet to pound home their need to be humble and focus on being a servant and not a lofty ruler in his kingdom, Judas leaves the room where they have shared the Passover meal, to betray Jesus to the authorities.

Jesus then explains he will be with them only a while longer (John 13:33). Here's how he puts it: "As I told the Jewish leaders, you will search for me, but you can't come where I am going" (NLT). Yet, a moment later Peter asks, "Lord, where are you going?" He'd told them many times that he was returning to the Father, so it's likely Peter isn't talking about heaven but a more local "trip." Obviously the disciples can't "search heaven" for Jesus, but he says they "will search" for him. The context implies Jesus is not talking about heaven either. He'll be arrested and taken away. They'll search the region for him, but he'll be sequestered, locked away, where they can't find him.

Let's go back to that Scripture in 1 Corinthians 15:23: "But there is an order to this resurrection: Christ was raised as the first of the harvest; then all who belong to Christ will be raised *when he comes back*" (NLT, italics mine). Paul makes clear no one is going to follow Jesus to heaven but, rather, when Jesus returns to reign on earth, he will then raise everyone—those faithful who are "asleep in death" and the unrighteous—to face a thousand years of Christ's reign, where they will be judged for their response to him as King of Kings.

So what was Jesus referring to when he spoke about where he was "going"? The context shows he is talking about the cross. He is about to give his life to redeem humanity, and that is a place—that cross on Calvary to die for the sins of humankind—that no one but he can go to.

How will Peter "follow [Jesus] later"? Peter will one day have his own cross to face, as history notes that he too was crucified.

When James and John approach Jesus on an earlier occasion, they say, "When you sit on your glorious throne, we want to sit in places of honor next to you, one on your right and the other on your left" (Mark 10:37 NLT—note, they don't specify this throne is in heaven). This follows:

> "You don't know what you are asking," Jesus said. "Can you drink the cup I drink or be baptized with the baptism I am baptized with?"
>
> "We can," they answered.
>
> Jesus said to them, "You will drink the cup I drink and be baptized with the baptism I am baptized with." (Mark 10:38–39 NIV)

Here we see Jesus telling these disciples plainly that they will indeed "drink" that cup of suffering for being his followers and be baptized into his death by dying as martyrs.

It's likely, therefore, that when Jesus tells Peter (and perhaps the others in the room as well) that they will follow him later, he is specifically talking about their martyrdom. Peter can't follow him now as Jesus goes to the cross, but they can follow in his footsteps later. Jesus told them plainly: "You will."

That this discussion is about his fate on the cross and not heaven is emphasized when Peter says, "Lord, why can't I follow you now? I will lay down my life for you" (verse 37). In other words, Peter is saying, if you are going to go die, I will go too and do likewise. So when Jesus then says, "You will follow me later," the context is clear: he's talking about following Jesus in *martyrdom*, not to a location in heaven. Context.

What Exactly Is "the Kingdom"?

I'd like to end this section on death and resurrection by clarifying something few Bible students consider. Scripture in numerous places does say we will "inherit the kingdom," but it doesn't say that by inheriting it we go live there—as if it's a place.

It's important to understand what the Greek word for kingdom—*basileia*—means and how it's used. It is not used the way we use it today, to mean a place, like the United Kingdom. Basileia means royalty, kingship, dominion, rule. As Strong's says of this word: "not to be confused with an actual kingdom but rather the right or authority to rule over a kingdom."[4]

This was mind-blowing to me when I first realized it, and I hope it is to you. Every time Jesus speaks of the kingdom of heaven, he is *not* describing what it's like in a place you should hope to go to one day. He is talking about what it will be like *living under his rule*. Pay attention to this as you study the gospels.

Everything will be so much clearer when you take the correct biblical perspective of this word, as you truly get what Jesus meant when he said to those around him: "The kingdom of God is within you [literally "in the midst of you is]" (Luke 17:21). *Entos*—within—is used only twice in the NT, in that passage in Luke and in Matthew 23:26, where Jesus admonishes the religious leaders to first "clean the inside of the cup" before the outside can be clean, referring to their insides, their hearts—which are within them (not in some place or location elsewhere). Jesus's power, authority, and rulership was standing right in their midst, and that's why he told them not to go looking elsewhere for it.

Why is this distinction important? Because believers need to stop thinking in terms of God's kingdom as a place—a place they are promised to dwell in someday. Believing that fallacy supports the unscriptural teaching that "all good people go to heaven."

Remember the 3 C's: context, consistency, character.

Now we can see more clearly what Jesus meant when he said, "Seek first the kingdom of God and his righteousness, and all these things will be added to you" (Matt 6:33 NKJV). He didn't mean for us to go looking for

---

4. Strong. *Concordance*, s.v. "Basileia," G932.

some heavenly abode or aspire to go live in heaven with God; he meant for us to submit to Jesus's *authority* as king, live righteously according to his kingdom principles. In Romans 14:7, Paul reiterates this: "The kingdom of God is not eating and drinking, but righteousness and joy and peace in the holy spirit" (NKJV). Paul obviously isn't talking about a place but about how we should behave under Jesus's rule and authority. Make sense?

"Men to Be Most Pitied"

First Corinthians 15:17–20 says this about Christ's resurrection:

> For if the dead do not rise, then Christ is not risen. And if Christ is not risen, your faith is futile; you are still in your sins! Then also those who have fallen asleep in Christ have perished. If in this life only we have hope in Christ, we are of all men the most pitiable. But now Christ is risen from the dead, and has become the firstfruits of those who have fallen asleep. (NKJV)

Think about this: if Jesus had stayed dead—a dead human—he would have perished and returned to the dust. Paul is saying that if that had taken place, then all humans would have the same fate. No door to eternal life would open. Jesus's resurrection ensures that believers won't end up as dust but will be gifted with immortality through redemption. Paul doesn't say Jesus is the firstfruits of *those who go to heaven*—note that. Only that he is the first to be raised of those who *have fallen asleep* to immortal life. Be careful not to add words into verses that are not there!

Jesus was the "last Adam," a perfect human equal to the first man. He had to be in order for Jesus to offer a propitiatory sacrifice—a life for a life. He was not some "half God, half man" while on earth. If he had been, he would not be exchanging an equal life for a life as required to fulfill the Law and God's requirement of justice (see 1 Cor 15:45). Paul explained to Timothy that there is "one God, and one mediator between God and men, *the man* Christ Jesus" (1 Tim 2:5 KJV, italics mine). This is important to understand because if Jesus was an Adam 2.0 version, then the argument some make that Jesus, being God on earth, could absorb all sin and evil in a single moment on the cross, but humans, being finite, would have to suffer for eternity to experience the requisite pain and suffering to equal Jesus's experience, might sound reasonable.

This is convoluted reasoning and unscriptural. He didn't have to suffer every sin in a few hours' time—the Law only required *an exact equal,* corresponding sacrifice—the death of a perfect man. That's why Jesus is called "the lamb of God that takes away the sin of the world" and portrays him as a lamb in Revelation, being worthy to receive all honor and authority because of his sacrifice (Rev 5:12; 13:8).

Yes, he nailed all our sins to the cross, and he suffered excruciating pain, and the reason he couldn't have been instantly slaughtered in a merciful way is that he had to experience a period of separation from God, which was demonstrated when he cried out, "My God, my God, why have you forsaken me?" (Matt 27:46 ESV). Why? Because God's eyes are said to be too pure to look upon sin (Hab 1:13). Jesus became sin for us (Gal 3:13). If God forsook the bearer of all sin, then sin could be erased, canceled out, just as the *azazel* goat was sent out of the camp to the wilderness to die with "all the sins of the people" on his head (Leviticus chapter 16). With a sin offering, it was required for the priest to first place his hands on the head of the blameless, "sinless" animal before it was slain to show that the animal would stand in place of the sinner(s). This action of sending away the sins of the people was how God blotted out their transgressions, and hence he remembered them no more (Isa 42:25).

If Christ hadn't been resurrected, humans would face the prospect of being dead forever. There is no immortal soul expressed here that survives death and goes on to experience some eternal existence elsewhere. Paul's words about "being men to be most pitied" is just one more nail in the coffin of the false doctrine of a human's inherent immortality.

PART 2: JUDGMENT

CHAPTER 12

Born Again for Salvation

ASK JUST ABOUT ANY Christian about salvation, and you'll hear phrases like "Once saved always saved" and "You must be born again to be saved." The topic of salvation is crucial to understand because it's tied up with judgment. Being saved means we are rescued from the penalty of sin, which is death.

It was never God's desire that his creation be subject to death. Death is called an enemy, and Christ vanquished this enemy by dying on the cross (1 Cor 15:26, 55) and ransoming us—paying the price of sin by becoming sin for us (Hos 13:14; 2 Cor 5:21). God has made only one way to salvation, and that's through belief in Jesus. Peter announced in Acts 4:12 that "there is no other name under heaven given to mankind by which we must be saved" (NIV). Indeed, "All the prophets testify about him that everyone who believes in him receives forgiveness of sins through his name" (Acts 10:43 NIV).

We've seen how those who die "in Christ," going to the grave already having accepted Christ Jesus as their covering for sin, have been given the right—not just the privilege—to be adopted as children of God. John 1:12 (ESV) says, "But to all who did receive him, who believed in his name, he gave the right to become children of God."

The Greek word used here for "right" is *exousia* and is often translated as "power." However, in this context it's likened to power of choice or permission. God extends welcome, permission, for believers to come into his family. With Jesus as the "second Adam" (1 Cor 15:45-49) and titled "Everlasting Father" (Isa 9:6) due to his purchasing us by his blood (1 Pet 1:18-19), we are sealed with the Holy Spirit, and God through Christ resides in us. In fact, Paul says to the Romans, "But you are not in the flesh but in the Spirit, if indeed the Spirit of God dwells in you. Now if anyone does not have the Spirit of Christ, he is not His" (Rom 8:9 NKJV).

Indeed, it is God's desire that everyone be saved. We read in 1 Thessalonians 5:9–10 (NKJV): "For God did not appoint us to wrath, but to obtain salvation through our Lord Jesus Christ, who died for us, that whether we wake or sleep, we should live together with Him" (*wake* and *sleep* being understood as euphemisms for being *alive* and *dead*).

Salvation is laid out simply. "If you declare with your mouth, 'Jesus is Lord,' and believe in your heart that God raised him from the dead, you will be saved" (Rom 10:9 NIV). When Paul and Silas were miraculously freed from their prison chains in Philippi, the jailer was terrified and asked, "Sirs, what must I do to be saved?" They replied, "Believe in the Lord Jesus, and you will be saved—you and your household" (Acts 16:30–31 NIV).

But all this raises some questions. Once you are saved by believing, adopted into God's family, and sealed with the Holy Spirit, does that mean you have been given a permanent pass into eternity? What did Jesus mean when he said in Matthew 12:32 (NIV), "Anyone who speaks a word against the Son of Man will be forgiven, but anyone who speaks against the Holy Spirit will not be forgiven, either in this age or in the age to come"? Can a saved believer lose his immortality card?

We get a hint about this unforgivable sin in the words of Stephen, right before he's martyred for his faith, when he accuses the religious leaders: "'You stiff-necked people! Your hearts and ears are still uncircumcised. You are just like your ancestors: You always resist the Holy Spirit!" (Acts 7:51 NIV). He goes on to accuse them of deliberately disobeying God's law (verse 53). In 1 John 3:8 we read: "Whoever makes a practice of sinning is of the devil, for the devil has been sinning from the beginning" (ESV).

The apostle Peter gives a scathing denunciation of the false teachers who were bringing in "destructive heresies" and denying Jesus (2 Pet 2:1 ESV), saying, "But these people blaspheme in matters they do not understand. They are like unreasoning animals, creatures of instinct, born only to be caught and destroyed, and like animals they too will perish" (verse 12 NIV). He then concludes this in verses 20–22:

> For if, after they have escaped the defilements of the world through the knowledge of our Lord and Savior Jesus Christ, they are again entangled in them and overcome, the last state has become worse for them than the first. For it would have been better for them

never to have known the way of righteousness than after knowing it to turn back from the holy commandment delivered to them. What the true proverb says has happened to them: "The dog returns to its own vomit, and the sow, after washing herself, returns to wallow in the mire."

These false teachers, who had once been saved—as confirmed by Peter's description of them having previously escaped the defilements of the world through their faith in Jesus—have sinned against the Holy Spirit. But it's not just false teachers that run the risk of ruin. The writer of Hebrews says this to those who are already saved:

> If we deliberately keep on sinning after we have received the knowledge of the truth, no sacrifice for sins is left, but only a fearful expectation of judgment and of raging fire that will consume the enemies of God. Anyone who rejected the law of Moses died without mercy on the testimony of two or three witnesses. How much more severely do you think someone deserves to be punished who has trampled the Son of God underfoot, who has treated as an unholy thing the blood of the covenant that sanctified them, and who has insulted the Spirit of grace? For we know him who said, "It is mine to avenge; I will repay," and again, "The Lord will judge his people." It is a dreadful thing to fall into the hands of the living God. (Heb 10:26–31 NIV)

Jude called those who had slipped into the church "wandering stars, for whom the gloom of utter darkness has been reserved forever" (verse 13 ESV).

We have to be careful about casting judgment on others, for only God can see a person's heart and know whether he or she is too far gone to respond to the prodding, even pleadings, of the Holy Spirit. But it's clear that salvation, while freely given as a gift of God's grace, has conditions. Even though we are under grace, Paul asks, "What then? Shall we sin because we are not under the law but under grace? By no means!" (Rom 6:15 NIV). Rather, he instructs us how to stay in God's favor and ensure our salvation: "Count yourselves dead to sin but alive to God in Christ Jesus. Therefore do not let sin reign in your mortal body so that you obey its evil desires. Do not offer any part of yourself to sin as an instrument of wickedness, but rather offer yourselves to God as those who have been brought from death to life; and offer every part of yourself to him as an instrument of righteousness" (verses 11–14).

We need to "work out [our] own salvation with fear and trembling" (Phil 2:12 NKJV). Not in fear of punishment but with a sober and serious realization that if we become a slave to sin, we fall out of God's favor. We've looked at Jesus's harsh words of condemnation that he will speak to those who claim to be his faithful followers when he returns to separate people into two camps (Matt 25:31–46). He will say to "many": "Get away from me; I never knew you" and states that those formerly "saved" believers will end up in the lake of fire, destroyed forever.

That judgment will come at the end of the thousand years of his reign, but it implies that while some believers might have formerly been in the group that will be raised up incorruptible, impervious to the final judgment—simply put, granted immortality upon their resurrection—instead these "goats" will be denied that privilege, which includes ruling on thrones and judging those resurrected. They will have to make some serious adjustments to be granted the gift of immortal life at the end of the thousand years.

CHAPTER 13

God's Judgment upon the World

WHO WOULD HAVE EVER imagined a simple fisherman would become such an erudite and imaginative writer? When I read Peter's letters, I'm in awe of the beautiful figurative and illustrative language he uses.

Let's take a moment to revisit this passage in 2 Peter chapter 2 because, to me, he sums up so clearly and expressively what the judgment of this world is all about. Simply put, we are to look at past examples of both God's judgment of the wicked and his deliverance of the righteous to know what lies ahead—because God never changes when it comes to his approach to handling sin.

After mentioning the influx of false teachers that will come in and corrupt the church, Peter states their "destruction [not eternal torment] has not been sleeping" (verse 3, NIV). This segues into his support of this claim (verses 4–9):

> For if God did not spare angels when they sinned, but sent them to hell [Greek: *tartaroo*], putting them in chains of darkness to be held for judgment; if he did not spare the ancient world when he brought the flood on its ungodly people, but protected Noah, a preacher of righteousness, and seven others; if he condemned the cities of Sodom and Gomorrah by burning them to ashes, and made them an example of what is going to happen to the ungodly; and if he rescued Lot, a righteous man, who was distressed by the depraved conduct of the lawless (for that righteous man, living among them day after day, was tormented in his righteous soul by the lawless deeds he saw and heard)—if this is so, then the Lord knows how to rescue the godly from trials and to hold the unrighteous for punishment on the day of judgment.

First, let me point out that Peter borrowed from the Greeks of his day by referring to a subterranean world they believed was the abode of the souls of wicked people called *tartaroo* or Tartarus. This word is used in the NT in this one verse only. The "chains of darkness" he refers to is the Greek word *zophos*, which is used five times in the NT to denote darkness or blackness (same word used in Homer's *Iliad* for the darkness of the netherworld). Because we know, as described in Revelation 20:7, that Satan will be let loose (freed, released) from his prison at the end of the thousand-year rule of Christ here on earth, and will then sway people to his side (and ultimately to share in his destruction in the lake of fire), it makes sense to describe these "fallen angels" allied with Satan as being in chains. Whether there is some form of actual chains in the spirit world, who knows. But the imagery is one we can easily understand.

As I mentioned right from the start, the teaching of immortality of the soul and said soul burning forever in a place of torment came from the Greeks, particularly the sect of the Gnostics, and this teaching, along with many others, filtered into the infant church in the first and second centuries. Gnostic philosophy, at the time of John's writing of Revelation, had infiltrated the Roman world. The Gnostics were a sect that combined elements of Christ's teaching with "mysteries" from other religions and performed secret rituals. Paul warned believers, in Colossians chapters 2 and 4, to beware of these types of persuasive and misleading teachings that might draw them away from the true knowledge, which is hidden in Christ alone (Col 2:3).

Note also Peter mentions that Sodom and Gomorrah (obviously meaning the people living in those towns) were condemned and so were burned to ash. He doesn't say the people there were sent to suffer eternal torment in hell. Their punishment was their death. They paid the price of their sin. And yet . . . as we noted earlier, Jesus said more than once that those inhabitants will "fare better" in the judgment (during the period of resurrection back to this earth in perfect human bodies) than many of Jesus's day. We can only presume that those who died in the great flood will also be resurrected to face judgment. Everyone God killed merely died. The fate of their soul—their eternal life—will depend on whether they accept or reject Jesus's kingship during his reign on earth during those thousand years. It will surely be an interesting time, to say the least!

So now that we've gotten a powerful argument from Peter convincing us that God knows how the punish the wicked and deliver the righteous

God's Judgment upon the World

from sin (and those wicked people), let's see what he next says about the fate of the heavens and earth.

Swinging back around to the example of Noah, we read in chapter 3 verses 3–12 (NIV):

> Above all, you must understand that in the last days scoffers will come, scoffing and following their own evil desires. They will say, "Where is this 'coming' he promised? Ever since our ancestors died, everything goes on as it has since the beginning of creation." But they deliberately forget that long ago by God's word the heavens came into being and the earth was formed out of water and by water. By these waters also the world of that time was deluged and destroyed. By the same word the present heavens and earth are reserved for fire, being kept for the day of judgment and destruction of the ungodly.
>
> But do not forget this one thing, dear friends: With the Lord a day is like a thousand years, and a thousand years are like a day. The Lord is not slow in keeping his promise, as some understand slowness. Instead he is patient with you, not wanting anyone to perish, but everyone to come to repentance.
>
> But the day of the Lord will come like a thief. The heavens will disappear with a roar; the elements will be destroyed by fire, and the earth and everything done in it will be laid bare.
>
> Since everything will be destroyed in this way, what kind of people ought you to be? You ought to live holy and godly lives as you look forward to the day of God and speed its coming. That day will bring about the destruction of the heavens by fire, and the elements will melt in the heat.

This passage is one that some uninformed Christians use to claim this planet, our earthly home, will literally be destroyed. Sadly, this belief, I feel, has caused many over the centuries to callously ignore humanity's charge of stewardship of our home and recklessly rape and pillage the earth with the excuse that "it's going to be burned up by God anyway."

We've learned that not only was the "earth given to the sons of man" as our dwelling place but it was also given to Jesus as his inheritance and possession (Ps 2:7–9)—and further in that psalm God warns the nations to serve the Lord with fear or suffer destruction (Hebrew: *abad*: perish, die, be put to death). Here on this earth, the faithful will join Jesus in ruling and judging all those resurrected (Rev 2:25–27; 5:9–10; 20:6).

Just as Jesus and the other New Testament writers believed and preached, Peter presented the only two choices available to any individual regarding future life prospects: death or life. He writes: "The Lord is not slow to fulfill his promise as some count slowness, but is patient toward you, not wishing that any should perish, but that all should reach repentance" (2 Pet 3:9 ESV. See also verse 7: "the *destruction* of ungodly men"). This echoes Christ's warning that "unless you repent you will all likewise perish" (Luke 13:3). Repent and be gifted immortal life or perish. Plain and simple.

Old Testament Metaphors That Depict the Fate of the Wicked

Edward Fudge, acclaimed theologian and lawyer, was called "one of the foremost scholars on hell," by the *Christian Post*.[1] Fudge's 1982 controversial book *The Fire That Consumes* did much to upend the traditional evangelical view of hell and torment.

He suggested people should look at the preponderance of evidence regarding the fate of the wicked the way a jury might. There are more than seventy metaphors and symbols depicting this fate, and Fudge notes these illustrative descriptions are, of course, not literal but they *correspond* to the reality. In other words, he says, once we witness the ultimate fate of the wicked at the end of the age, we would agree and say, "Yes, that fits what God told us in advance would happen."

Here is a partial list of how verses in the Psalms depict this eventuality:

> 37:2: wither like grass; grass cut down
> 1:4: chaff blown away
> 58:8: snail that melts
> 68:2: wax that melts
> 2:9 clay pot that is broken
> 58:7: water that flows away
> 68:2: smoke that vanishes
> 83:13: stubble blown away
> 110:5–6: heaping up of the dead (corpses)

In every instance of metaphor regarding the eventual fate of the wicked, we get a sense of destruction or nonexistence. Never one of torment. In addition, the Hebrew Scriptures have more than fifty verbs, passive and active, that describe this fate, and none of them are about pain, torture, or suffering.

---

1. Vu, "Interview," line 2.

Hosea 13:3 states: "They shall be like the morning mist or like the dew that goes early away, like the chaff that swirls from the threshing floor or like smoke from a window" (KJV). These comparisons of the fate of the wicked with the morning mist, early dew, chaff swirling from the floor, and the smoke are consistently showing a disappearance. Evildoers will disappear from God's earth, and we will look for them, but they will be no more (Ps 37:10).

Jesus's Use of Metaphor to Describe the Fate of the Wicked

Jesus often used metaphor, parables, or current events to paint a picture of what awaited the wicked. Here are some of his illustrative comparisons:

Unfaithful tenants who are killed (Luke 20:16)

An evil servant who is cut in pieces (Matt 24:51)

Those destroyed by the Great Flood (Luke 17:27)

The inhabitants of Sodom and Gomorrah destroyed by fire and brimstone (Luke 17:29)

Rebellious servants killed when their master returns (Luke 19:14, 27)

Galileans who died at Pilate's hand (Luke 13:2–3)

Eighteen people crushed by a tower (Luke 13:4–5)

Many of these examples imply capital punishment—death. After telling the parable about the unfaithful tenants, Jesus asked: "When the owner of the vineyard comes, what will he do to those vinedressers?" His listeners replied, "He will destroy those wicked men miserably, and lease his vineyard to other vinedressers who will render to him the fruits in their seasons." (Matt 21:40 NKJV). Jesus confirmed their answer by compounding it with these words: "Therefore I say to you, the kingdom of God will be taken from you and given to a nation bearing the fruits of it. And whoever falls on this stone will be broken; but on whomever it falls, it will grind him to powder" (verses 43–44). Nothing about being tortured in fire forever. No, those who reject Jesus will be destroyed, as if ground to powder.

God's judgment is eternal, but it is also merciful and swift. In Ezekiel 33:11, we read: "As I live, declares the Lord God, I have no pleasure in the death of the wicked, but that the wicked turn from his way and live" (ESV).

That should make us love and adore our Father all the more, knowing he would never prolong anyone's sentence of judgment just to see that person suffer.

CHAPTER 14

"Wrath and Fury" and "Weeping and Gnashing of Teeth"

THE BIBLE USES EXPRESSIONS such as "wrath and fury" and "weeping and gnashing of teeth" when talking about the punishment of the wicked. Ah, surely these expressions provide the absolute proof that the wicked suffer torment after they die, no?

Well, we've already learned that nothing remains after death. There is no immortal soul, no disembodied soul, no conscious "spirit" that can feel or experience anything—neither pleasure nor pain. So if the wicked are foretold to suffer God's wrath and fury, and engage in weeping and gnashing of teeth, what does that all mean?

The apostle Paul, after laying out the basic truth that God "will render to every man according to his deeds" (Rom 2:6 NKJV), goes on to explain the two possible "renderings":

> To those who by patience in well-doing seek for glory and honor and immortality, he will give eternal life; but for those who are self-seeking and do not obey the truth, but obey unrighteousness, there will be wrath and fury. There will be tribulation and distress for every human being who does evil. (verses 7–9 ESV)

Wow, tribulation and distress. Sounds like a lot of suffering. First off: context! Note in that passage it's only those who are faithful who get immortality—eternal life. Those disobedient to God experience wrath and fury, words connected with the final judgment (Rev 14:10; 16:19). Paul is probably harkening to Zephaniah's description of "the Day of the Lord" (which is synonymous with that judgment "day") in which God will consume the world with "the fire of his jealous wrath" and cause "distress and anguish" (Zeph 1:15, 18). But note, too, what the prophet says the result will be: "a sudden end of all who live in the earth."

Of course God isn't speaking about every single human on the earth because—as you have clearly seen—the entire body of Scripture makes it clear that it's only the wicked who will be removed so that you will look for his place and he won't be found (Ps 37:10). Jesus noted that while one would be taken, another would be left (behind, remain—Luke 17:34–35). The goats go into everlasting punishment—a sentence of punishment that will never be reversed—but the sheep inherit the kingdom prepared for them from the founding of the world. Where will that kingdom be? On earth. The meek sheep inherit the earth (Matt 5:5). Let's not make this complicated! Zephaniah no doubt was speaking about an end of all the wicked—those to whom the Day of the Lord causes distress.

Paul on numerous occasions contrasts those "who are being saved [Greek: *hoi sozomenoi*]" and "those who are perishing [*hoi apollumenoi*]" (1 Cor 1:18; 2 Cor 2:15; 4:3; 2 Thess 2:10). Pay attention: what's contrasted with salvation is "perishing," not torture. While God has the right to do whatever he wants with his creation, he gave us free will, and that means he respects the choice or options he's put before all humanity. As I mentioned early on, God wants his creation to love, appreciate, respect, and honor him. And who could sincerely do that if the threat of torture was being dangled over one's head?

Let's see what the Bible says about these "agonies" unbelievers will suffer. The expression "weeping and gnashing of teeth" occurs seven times in the New Testament, some of these instances in Jesus's parables.

Edward Fudge makes a nice point: "Throughout the Bible, gnashing of teeth expresses not pain but rage [Job 16:9; Ps 35:16; Lam 2:16, to cite a few]. . . . But even while this wicked man (Ps 112:10) grinds his teeth, he wastes away and comes to nothing."[1]

There are seven Scriptures in the NT that speak of weeping and gnashing of teeth, and in some of these instances this behavior is accompanied by those sufferers being thrown into darkness, thrown away, assigned a place with the hypocrites, and weeded out of the kingdom. Every instance is tied to some description of banishment (never torture).

Fudge says, "Weeping indicates sorrow, as the doomed begin to realize that God has thrown them out as worthless and as they begin to recognize

---

1. Fudge, *The Fire That Consumes*, 158.

"Wrath and Fury" and "Weeping and Gnashing of Teeth"

the immanence of their own upcoming permanent demise. Throughout the Bible, gnashing of teeth always expresses rage, here toward God who sentenced them, and toward the redeemed, who forever will be blessed."[2]

Acts 7:54 says that when Stephen accused those listening to him of crucifying Jesus, "they were cut to the quick, and they began gnashing their teeth at him" (NASB).

How long the unrighteous must linger "outside in the dark" in the knowledge that they are going to be destroyed, the Bible doesn't say. But this is what the wicked will experience, rather than be suddenly destroyed without knowing why or that God is punishing them. This judgment is compared to Noah's day, and back when Noah was building the ark, he was "a herald of righteousness" to the ungodly world (2 Pet 2:5). It can be assumed that when the floodwaters were unleashed, there was a period of time—perhaps quite brief—when these ungodly realized their demise and, perhaps, wept and gnashed their teeth at Noah and God.

At the final judgment, at the end of the thousand-year reign of Christ on earth, before the wicked are destroyed in the lake of fire, they will know they have made an irreversible choice. God has always urged people to "choose life so that you may live," but he forces no one to make either choice (Deut 30:19). While some will express rage and fury toward God for this judgment, perhaps terror and grief, those emotions will be momentary, for once they are no longer alive, their love and hate and all other feelings will disappear along with their lives (Eccl 9:6).

Another facet of this is the witness God wants to give the righteous. The Bible repeatedly speaks of how they will look on and see the demise of the ungodly (Ps 37:34; 58:10). Thousands will fall around the righteous, but God tells them, "You will only observe with your eyes and see the punishment of the wicked" (Ps 91:8 NIV).

---

2. Fudge, *The Fire That Consumes*, 158.

CHAPTER 15

Judgment—Sooner and Later

WE KNOW WITHOUT A doubt that God will judge the world, and it will be a righteous judgment (Ps 9:7–8). The apostle Paul in Acts 17:31 says, "For he has set a day when he will judge the world with justice by the man he has appointed. He has given proof of this to everyone by raising him from the dead" (NIV). What does Paul mean by "a day"? Well, let's start digging into the Scriptures and see.

Romans 2:5–11 shows us how God plans to judge:

> But because of your stubbornness and your unrepentant heart, you are storing up wrath against yourself for the day of God's wrath, when his righteous judgment will be revealed. God will repay each person according to what they have done. To those who by persistence in doing good seek glory, honor and immortality, he will give eternal life. But for those who are self-seeking and who reject the truth and follow evil, there will be wrath and anger. There will be trouble and distress for every human being who does evil: first for the Jew, then for the Gentile; but glory, honor and peace for everyone who does good: first for the Jew, then for the Gentile. For God does not show favoritism. (NIV)

We see in this passage that God doesn't show favoritism, and perhaps the Jews in Rome felt they'd get some special treatment or a pass because of their nation's prior covenant relationship with God. But Paul points out each person will face Jesus in the judgment and have to account for what they've done. In 2 Corinthians 5:10, we read similarly: "For we must all appear before the judgment seat of Christ, so that each of us may receive what is due us for the things done while in the body, whether good or bad" (NIV). John 5:22 tells us God has handed over all the responsibility

Judgment—Sooner and Later

of judging "to the Son." And we saw earlier how, upon Jesus's return, he will separate people, "sheep" from "goats," and those of each group will go their appointed ways—either into eternal life or eternal destruction (Matt 25:31–46).

Jesus will judge both "the living and the dead" (Acts 10:42), and we understand the dead get judged by being first made alive again, in human bodies on earth during the period of the resurrection of the dead. We also clearly saw from the Bible that no one is raised to heaven in some spirit form to get judged. Jesus explained in no uncertain terms that the dead would be raised from their graves, whether they died on land or in the sea, and face him.

This is where things get a bit dicey. A whole lot of theologians and Bible students believe that the moment the dead are raised, which they say is at the end of Jesus's one-thousand-year reign on earth, they are brought before the throne, judged, and then are cast into the lake of fire, where they will suffer eternally, weeping and gnashing their teeth (which you now understand means annihilation, not torment, and the weeping and gnashing is *before* that destruction).

All the dead are to be raised and judged, yet we are told more than once by Jesus himself that those who lived in Sodom and Gomorrah back in the day, who committed atrocities worth divine retribution, will not only be resurrected but will "fare better" than those who disbelieved Jesus when he walked the earth.

This is very important to pay attention to. It tells us judgment isn't a "one and done" type of pronouncement. You aren't raised up, told your former sins were really bad so you merit destruction, then sent off to your fate.

Daniel 12:2 says: "Multitudes who sleep in the dust of the earth will awake: some to everlasting life, others to shame and everlasting contempt" (NIV). It's hard to conceive of those who will awake (from death) to face shame and contempt—to experience it—if they are instantly sent off to some realm of torment. Immortal "souls" burning in some fire wouldn't have others around them expressing contempt or shaming them. But if they coexist with the righteous "made perfect" and have to work to turn swords into pruning shears and learn war no more, under the watchful eye of the kings and priests who rule with Christ for a thousand years . . . well, there are surely going to be periods of shame and everlasting contempt experienced by those who refuse to accept Christ's rule.

Hell No

The Thousand-Year Reign of Christ

Jesus is going to reign on the earth for a thousand years once he returns. But whom will he reign over? Many believe this to be only those who turned to Christ during the tribulation and became believers (and some claim that group is made up of only converted Jews). All the believers before that are supposedly hanging out in heaven in spirit bodies (for the time being). This supposes *only* those saved *during that short period of seven years* alone would benefit from Christ's rule, and at the end of the thousand years, all the "bad" people (many of whom never heard of Jesus because he hadn't been born yet when they were alive) would be brought to life, only to be sentenced to hellfire for eternity immediately after.

I hope you see how crazy and unjust this sounds. Why would *only* people who live during a seven-year period in human history—out of more than six thousand years—get the privilege of living under Christ's rule for a thousand years? Does that make any sense? In contrast to those very few lucky ones, all those who lived before them don't get the chance to benefit from the kingdom and the teachings that flow from his throne. Yet . . . somehow there are nations during the thousand-year reign—warring nations that must stop fighting and "learn war no more." Are those only the small group of saved tribulation Jews? How can that be if they are numerous nations in conflict? Let's put on our thinking caps and use some of the brains God gave us to figure this out.

> And I saw an angel coming down from heaven, having the key of the abyss and a great chain in his hand. And he laid hold of the dragon, the serpent of old, who is the devil and Satan, and bound him for a thousand years, and threw him into the abyss, and shut it and sealed it over him, so that he should not deceive *the nations* any longer, until the thousand years were completed; after these things he must be released for a short time. And I saw thrones, and they sat upon them, and judgment was given to them. And I saw the souls of those who had been beheaded because of the testimony of Jesus and because of the word of God, and those who had not worshiped the beast or his image, and had not received the mark upon their forehead and upon their hand; and they came to life and reigned with Christ for a thousand years. (Rev 20:1–4 NASB, italics mine)

So here we see faithful followers of Christ reigning with him for a thousand years—which implies someone to reign over. There is no reason to believe this number is symbolic of some other number. Paul talks about Christ (1 Cor 15:24–26) reigning *until he puts all enemies under his feet*. And the last enemy mentioned is death—which we know will be done away with once the unfaithful are symbolically thrown into the lake of fire. After that, no one anywhere will ever die because all those who chose to be faithful to Jesus will be granted immortality.

Now, if there are "enemies" to be put underfoot *during* the thousand years, and we are told that at the *end* of the thousand years Satan will not only be loosed from his "prison" but will go out and deceive *nations* in all four corners of the earth (Rev 20:7–8), that tells us that the thousand-year rule of peace on earth is going to be an interesting time—with a world full of people—whole nations—who may not be all that happy or obedient to Jesus. We are told in Isaiah 2:2–4 (NIV) that

> in the last days
> the mountain of the Lord's temple will be established
>   as the highest of the mountains;
> it will be exalted above the hills,
>   and all nations will stream to it.
>
> Many peoples will come and say,
> "Come, let us go up to the mountain of the Lord,
>   to the temple of the God of Jacob.
> He will teach us his ways,
>   so that we may walk in his paths."
> The law will go out from Zion,
>   the word of the Lord from Jerusalem.
> He will judge between the nations
>   and will settle disputes for many peoples.
> They will beat their swords into plowshares
>   and their spears into pruning hooks.
> Nation will not take up sword against nation,
>   nor will they train for war anymore.

We can be sure that the "last days" aren't pertaining to this current world system because Jesus first has to come and take the throne on earth. We have never seen anyone on a throne in Jerusalem judge nations in such a way that they will not engage in war ever again (which is what *anymore* means). Here we see that during this reign there will still be "nations" that will be having disputes. Yet, Jesus will judge "between nations" and settle disputes in his role as judge and king. A judge doesn't merely pass a final judgment on someone; judges give instruction, direction, and laws to be followed.

When Jesus rules on his throne on earth, he will require people to stop warring and be peaceful. I can imagine how many people, from all times in history, will resist his ways of peace. Isaiah chapter 65 paints a picture of this time, stating that not only will there be a "new heavens and a new earth" but the former things will not be remembered (verse 17—Revelation mentions pain, suffering, mourning, and outcry will be gone) and that we should "be glad and rejoice forever in what [God] creates." We then read about the resulting idyllic conditions: "The wolf and the lamb will feed together, and the lion will eat straw like the ox, and dust will be the serpent's food. They will neither harm nor destroy on all my holy mountain" (verse 25, NIV).

Some teach that the righteous will be in heaven during that time (and even forever), while only the wicked will be stuck on earth to suffer the wrath of Jesus's reign, with the 144,000 faithful ruling alongside him. But, as we've seen, no one goes to heaven. Only the Son of Man, who came from heaven, ascended there—ever (John 3:13). And since the righteous are to rise first—those asleep in Christ—we have the picture of this planet earth first populated with those who survive the Great Tribulation, faithful and unfaithful, and the risen dead "in Christ." After those in Christ are raised up—who knows how long a time period this covers—everyone in their graves all the way back to the first family will be brought back to life—a life of judgment—and some will "fare better" during that thousand years than others.

Remember, God intended for this planet to become a paradise full of creatures, and he intended for perfect humans to fill the earth and subdue it. His word never, ever, goes forth without accomplishing the results he intended. God didn't, at some point, look at sinful humans in surprise and then decide to change his mind. He didn't look at the situation here on earth once sin entered, as if he had no clue this would happen, and decide to alter his plan and have humans get changed into some kind of spirit form and live in heaven with him. We've seen how incontrovertible the Scriptures are in their consistent teaching that humans were made for the earth—given the earth as their possession—but heaven belongs to God. Let's always keep this truth in mind.

Jesus spoke repeatedly of raising people up "in the last day" (John 5:25–29; 6:39–40, 54). Hence, this "day of resurrection" is when people will be brought back to life.

The Millennium Is a Literal Thousand Years

Some argue that the one-thousand-year reign of Christ is merely figurative, that Jesus isn't actually going to rule on earth for that length of time. One Bible researcher I spoke to wrote me: "I am worried that if people (good and bad) are taught they are raised to live during a literal thousand-year period on earth after Christ's return, then this seems, among other things, to give people false hope of some kind of 'second chance' contrary to Hebrews 9:27."

He wondered how I could take this time period as literal when Revelation is highly symbolic.

Let's break this down. There are five verses in Revelation that mention these thousand years (Rev 20:2–7). One might think the repetition alone would hint at being literal. But that's not a weighty factor to conclusively claim a literal interpretation. In these passages we're told that the dragon (devil) is bound for the full thousand years so he can't mislead anyone during that period, then the first resurrection takes place and the faithful sit on thrones to rule and judge with Jesus. Then, when the thousand years have ended, Satan is released from his prison to mislead nations in a final testing of humanity.

While Hebrews 9:27 says it's appointed for humans to die once, to pay the price for sin, followed by "judgment," there is nothing here that prevents this judgment period from being one thousand years long. And how can this be a false hope of a "second chance" when the majority of mankind hasn't been given a "first chance" to know the truth about Jesus? I keep pointing to God's character—a just God would not punish billions of people just because they lived before Jesus walked the earth, or lived in a place and/or situation that didn't allow for them to hear the gospel. Should people be tormented in fire forever because of that? Should they even be deprived of the chance of conferred immortality because of something that was no fault of their own? Luck of the draw? We know our just God would never operate that way.

How much time would you guess it would take to resurrect the billions of humans that have lived on this earth and teach them Jesus's ways, with the appointed judges/kings on their thrones ruling with Jesus and directing the fulfillment of God's purpose on this earth—to fill and subdue it with humans who all know the Lord as the waters cover the seas? Surely it would take some time.

Let me point out something that I feel is significant and answers this literal/symbolic question decisively. God, the creator of time, *never* uses time loosely in prophecy. Some of the more than two thousand prophecies in the Bible have specific time periods allocated. All the Old Testament prophecies that foretold events to occur within or by a certain time were fulfilled to the day.

While I don't have room to elaborate on every single prophecy, I'll refer to a few, and you can do your own investigation. This may get a bit deep.

Daniel 9:25-26 foretold when the Messiah would appear. In 458 BC, Persian King Artaxerxes gave the decree to rebuild Jerusalem. Daniel prophesied this shortly before 500 BC. With calendar adjustments (switching from the Anno Mundi calendar to the one Dionysius came up with and keeping in mind there is no "zero" year between 1 BC and AD 1), most historians settle on around AD 26 as the start of Jesus's ministry. The prophecy also notes that the Messiah would be "cut off" or killed at half a week (of years), or three and a half years. This is perhaps the most widely known "time-stamped" prophecy in the OT. Fulfilled exactly as prophesied.

In Ezekiel chapter 4, that prophet is told to lie on his side for 390 days to represent the number of years of Israel's sin (the northern ten-tribe split-off kingdom) and then 40 days for the years of Judah's sin (the two-tribe kingdom and capital, verses 4-8). These are years of punishment for the respective kingdoms (verse 4 makes this clear).

The first punishment of forty years, when Israel wandered in the wilderness, took place between 1445 and 1406 BC. In Leviticus 26:3-13, God lays out the blessings the next generations will face upon entering the Promised Land *if* they keep his commands. But ... verses 14-17 warn what the punishment will be if they disobey, and they're harsh.

We read in Leviticus 26:18: "And after all this, if you [Israel] do not obey Me, then I will punish you seven times more for your sins" (NKJV—see also verses 19-20). God would punish Israel by removing the inhabitants from the land for a period "seven times more" than the originally stated punishment if they didn't turn from their wicked ways. Those 40 days, which stood for 40 years, when multiplied by seven is 280 years. In 721 BC, Assyria invaded the capital city of the northern ten-tribe kingdom of Israel and Samaria fell, and the residents were hauled away (2 Kgs 18:10). Then, in 445 BC, King Artaxerxes issued that decree to have Jerusalem be built once again—ending the prophetic period of punishment (Neh 2:1–8). Exactly 280 years.

This wasn't a loose time prediction. It was specific to the year. God didn't have Ezekiel lie on one side for however many days he felt like it. God gave him specific numbers that represented specific prophetic years. God, the maker and keeper of time itself, uses time in exact ways in the Bible. There are plenty of Scriptures you can research that show this fact.

Hence, there is no good scriptural reason to think the thousand years in Revelation is figurative or has already begun in heaven in some nebulous way, as many claim. Jesus laid out a series of events that must take place in order, including seven literal years of a great tribulation, 1,290 days (3.5 years) before the abomination of desolation occurs, and 42 months for the antichrist to rule (Rev 13:5). Daniel's "half week" of 3.5 years was literal, so why wouldn't Revelation's be? Why give specific time lengths in a figurative or symbolic fashion? If they're not exact measurements of time, why not just have the apostle John say "for a while" or "for some months"?

It's hard, if not impossible, to wrangle Scriptures to support the belief that the thousand-year reign of Christ is actually not the thousand-year reign of Christ. It's interesting to note that, to God, a thousand years is like one day (2 Pet 3:8), and Paul talks about a "day" in which God will judge the inhabited earth by Jesus (Acts 17:31). God told Adam that in that "day" he eats from the forbidden tree, he will die. Adam died at the age of 930, within a "thousand-year day" (Gen 5:5). God himself gives us this math in the Bible, the equation of a day (to God) = one thousand years. Therefore, it's biblical to consider the thousand-year reign of Christ as a literal Judgment "Day."

Resurrection and Marriage

Another interesting tidbit Jesus gave us via the gospels (and this conversation is noted in three gospels—Matt 22:23–31; Mark 12:18–27; Luke 20:27–40), yet leaves us with a lot of questions, is the discussion he has with the Sadducees, a sect of the Jews (mentioned earlier, who didn't believe in the resurrection) about marriage. We read in Matthew 22 of one of these asking Jesus whom a woman would be married to in the resurrection after having been married to seven different men during her lifetime. The

Sadducee asks, "Therefore, in the resurrection, whose wife will she be? For they all had her" (verse 28, NKJV). Jesus answers:

> "You are mistaken, not knowing the Scriptures nor the power of God. For in the resurrection they neither marry nor are given in marriage, but are like angels of God in heaven. But concerning the resurrection of the dead, have you not read what was spoken to you by God, saying, 'I am the God of Abraham, the God of Isaac, and the God of Jacob'? God is not the God of the dead, but of the living." (verses 29–32)

An intriguing statement, right? Since we know that Abraham, Isaac, and Jacob were and are "asleep with their forefathers," why did Jesus say they were living? Luke 20:38 (NKJV) puts it this way: "For He is not the God of the dead but of the living, for all live to him."

Ah, here's some clarity (and why it's so important to follow the rule of the 3 C's, to see the consistency among all relevant verses). Why are these ancient honored Jews called "alive" by Jesus? Because they live *to God*—or, to put it another way, in God's eyes, his estimation, all who are called "dead" are alive because they are merely sleeping, awaiting Jesus's call to wake from "sleep" in the resurrection. Just in the way this is worded, we are shown they didn't go to heaven upon their deaths in some spirit form. If they had been, Jesus wouldn't have used that phrase "all live to him." He would have, instead, said something like "for all are now living in heaven." Remember—God is outside of time. They are already alive in the future—where we will be one day and where we will meet these patriarchs. These powerful leaders were mistaken about Scripture because they believed no one would ever be resurrected, punished, or held accountable for their actions, and they even rejected the belief in angels or demons.[1] They truly did not know the very Scriptures they claimed to be authorities on, nor did they acknowledge the power of God—his ability to raise people from the dead.

But let's get back to the meat of that passage about the resurrection. Jesus didn't say humans who are resurrected *will be angels* in heaven. They will be *like* angels—and in one specific way. Not because they exist in a spirit realm and have spirit bodies. Jesus isn't talking about that at all. He's discussing marriage. And, like angels, resurrected humans will not marry during the thousand years and beyond.

Why is that? Does that mean we can't be with a spouse we love dearly? Does that mean families will no longer exist? No more sex? Will God

---

1. Philipson-Samoscz. *The Jewish Encyclopedia*, 631.

eliminate the desire for mating and having children? Will he consider the earth "full" so that it needs no further filling?

Good questions. And the Bible does not answer them. But we do know one thing: God is a God of love. It makes no sense that he would raise us all up in "the last day" and not allow us to be with our family members. At this juncture, how "things" will work on earth during Christ's reign and beyond is a black box that we cannot open on this side of paradise. But we can trust that the God who made us in his image and knows the plans he has for us, to give us that future and a hope (Jer 29:11), will bring us complete joy, happiness, and fulfillment in his presence when we "see his face" (Rev 22:4—cf. Matt 5:8). Just as when Adam was in the garden of Eden, and God "walked" with him each day, communing with him, so too God will be with us and wipe every tear from our eye (Rev 21:4). I don't know about you, but I'm not going to get tripped up over how my husband and I will relate to each other in the kingdom. I trust God has it all worked out so we will be truly happy.

Let me conclude by mentioning there have been some large camps over the years that proclaimed the millennium has already taken place or that we're already in it, and, if it interests you, you can find plenty of articles and books online that share those arguments. Some claim this separating of "sheep and goats" has been an ongoing event into our time. But there is no reason to go there because of what the Bible so clearly shows.

Daniel 2:44 speaks of the arrival of Christ's kingdom causing the destruction of every government on earth before Jesus takes the throne. That hasn't happened. Peter speaks of the Day of the Lord basically burning up the entire human governmental and societal machine (2 Pet 3:10). Paul says that when Jesus returns, when he is "revealed from heaven," it will be in blazing fire with his powerful angels" (2 Thess 1:6–7). And Jesus himself said he will come with the clouds accompanied by all the angels of heaven (Matt 25:31). And so on. It's clear the millennium has not begun, and Jesus has not returned in his glory to rule.

Yes, right now he has all the power and authority, granted to him by the Father upon his victory over the cross and death. But there is an appointed time for Jesus to return and take the throne and rule over the nations, which, the psalmist says, will be "with an iron rod." Read all of Psalm 2 to see how clearly God speaks of installing Jesus on his holy mountain and how his seated King will "dash them to pieces like pottery" (verse 9 NIV).

CHAPTER 16

The Dead Who "Do Not Come to Life" until the End

IT'S A PREVALENT TEACHING in churches that the resurrection of unbelievers to "judgment" will not occur until the full thousand years of Christ's reign have run out. At that time, they state, the unrighteous will be raised from death, given a speedy sentence, and whisked off to eternal torment. The singular Scripture this is based on is Revelation 20:5, where we read, "But the rest of the dead did not live again until the thousand years were finished" (NKJV).

Let's look at the full passage to put this in context:

> And I saw thrones, and they sat on them, and judgment was committed to them. Then I saw the souls of those who had been beheaded for their witness to Jesus and for the word of God, who had not worshiped the beast or his image, and had not received his mark on their foreheads or on their hands. And they lived and reigned with Christ for a thousand years.
>
> But the rest of the dead did not live again until the thousand years were finished. This is the first resurrection. Blessed and holy is he who has part in the first resurrection. Over such the second death has no power, but they shall be priests of God and of Christ, and shall reign with Him a thousand years. (verses 4–7)

The emphasis here is on the *first* resurrection, of the faithful—those who were martyred for their faith, including those who suffered during the Great Tribulation. A distinction is made between those participating in this first resurrection and "the rest of the dead" who "did not live again" until the end of Christ's reign on earth.

The Dead Who "Do Not Come to Life" until the End

Other translations say "lived not again" or "did not come to life." If we look at the phrase in Greek, we see two words for *lived not again*: *anazao* and *uo* (no or not).

Anazao is used five times in the Bible and can mean live again, recover life, be restored to a correct life, return to a better moral state, and to revive or regain strength and vigor, according to Strong's definition.[1] The other four instances of this word are found in Luke 15:24, 32 and Romans 7:9 and 14:9. The first references in Luke apply to the parable of the prodigal son, in which the father declares his son, who was figuratively dead and has now returned home, is now figuratively alive. In Romans we see another figurative usage with Paul declaring, "I was alive once without the law, but when the commandment came, sin revived and I died." The only literal usage of this word is in the last reference, when Paul states: "For to this end Christ died and rose and lived again, that he might be Lord of both the dead and the living" (NKJV).

This leaves a fuzzy path ahead regarding those dead who "did not live again" until the judgment period is over. Do we take this word in Revelation 20:5 to mean the *moment* of resurrection? Or do we take this as the *condition* or declaration of living? In other words, Jesus didn't just rise and was alive again in one singular moment; he came to life in that he was, upon his resurrection, forever in the *state* of being alive, going forward.

Since all five instances could be construed in the same way, why wouldn't we presume that latter understanding? The dead who are raised do not "come to life" or are granted endless, eternal life until the end of the thousand years, at the moment they face the final judgment. That doesn't mean they are dead in the dust up until that moment. It means while they have been alive on earth under Jesus's rule, they are not considered "alive again" or to have "come into life" or have immortality conferred upon them until Jesus reads from the Book of Life—and only if their names are in said book. The "rest of the dead" who are going to join those granted immortality in the first resurrection won't get issued this "eternal life card" alongside them until the end of the thousand years.

I always swing back to the times Jesus spoke of the inhabitants of Sodom faring better in the resurrection. How can this be so if they are merely to be raised up at the end of the thousand years, told they are wicked, and pitched into the lake of fire? It makes no sense. What makes more sense is that all will be raised up at the start of the millennium, with those asleep

1. Strong, *Concordance*, s.v. "Anazao," G326

in Christ raised first, followed by those "not in Christ," who will have that period of time to listen to the law going forth from the throne and get with Jesus's program to "learn war no more," for Jesus is hailed as the Prince of Peace, and surely he isn't presently in that role or has been in any time in history. Isaiah 9:7 says, "Of the increase of his government and of peace there will be no end, on the throne of David and over his kingdom, to establish it and to uphold it with justice and with righteousness from this time forth and forevermore. The zeal of the LORD of hosts will do this" (ESV). As the enthroned Prince of Peace, he will require nations to settle disputes and turn their swords into pruning shears—something we have not yet seen fulfilled but will—because every promise of God is yes and amen in Christ Jesus (2 Cor 1:20).

Yes, this is difficult theology. It's challenging to parse out the meanings and pieces. But, like a puzzle, you can't force any piece into a space that is the wrong shape, and that's what so many Bible scholars and students do. All I'm trying to do is encourage you to make sure you are putting the right pieces in the right places and creating the exact picture the Bible portrays—so long as the Bible gives us all the pieces. There are some answers we are just going to have to wait for—like why God created dinosaurs and leeches. Well, I have my own unique questions for God!

Many scholars teach the wicked are resurrected at the end of the thousand years because that's when they'll be "judged." Hence, they reason, the resurrection of the "saved" begins at the beginning of the thousand years. Yet, while these scholars say the righteous are raised to heaven, they don't say who actually will be on earth, whom the 144,000 kings and judges will rule over and judge. Why have kings and judges—and so many!—if no one's there to be ruled and judged?

One Long Judgment Day

Since Paul and Jesus spoke of one particular "day" and one specific resurrection—a day coming in which *all* the dead will rise from their graves, some to everlasting life and others to judgment—why would we conclude there are multiple "judgment days"? Yes, the dead in Christ rise first, then those "not in Christ" (all who never knew of him or had but did not acknowledge him as their savior) would rise after—including those who personally knew him back in Israel when he walked the earth.

The Dead Who "Do Not Come to Life" until the End

It's clear those raised in Christ have proven their loyalty and aren't subject to the second death. They don't have to "come to life" or be granted eternal life at the end of the thousand years because they've already earned their crown and "the second death has no power over them." Remember what Revelation 20:4 says: "Those who had not worshiped the beast or his image, and had not received the mark upon their forehead and upon their hand; and they came to life and reigned with Christ for a thousand years" (NASB). There's that phrase again—"come to life." Believers in Christ "come to life"—get immortality conferred upon them—the moment they are resurrected. But the wicked do not. They must prove their faithfulness over a thousand years, then, when the books are opened and their works examined, the Great Judge will grant them to "come to life" if they've proven worthy.

A good reason to accept Christ now, in this time of salvation (2 Cor 6:2). Jesus said, "Most assuredly, I say to you, he who hears My word and believes in him who sent Me has everlasting life, and shall not come into judgment, but has passed from death into life" (John 5:24 NKJV). Those who die in Christ, then "sleep in Christ," will be raised up incorruptible, never to die again. They have passed from the condemnation of death by sharing in Christ's death, burial, and resurrection (Rom 6:3–8; Col 2:12–13). They "shall not come into [adverse] judgment."

But think carefully here. If we accept the interpretation—which is not supported by the other uses of the word anazao (come to life, live again)—and believe no one but the righteous will be resurrected until the end of the thousand years, then who on earth—literally—will be ruled over? Who will make up those warring nations that Christ will instruct? Who will learn war no more? This has not happened yet, so it is a future event. And this process of "turning swords into pruning shears" is to take place under kingdom rule on earth.

Doesn't it make much more sense and seem consistent with context and all other Scripture that *all the dead* will hear Jesus's voice, be raised to life on earth, and live under his rule—with the faithful getting the honored positions of priest and king and being raised up incorruptible (not subject to the second death)?

Sure, it's going to be a tough millennial for some—those who resist Jesus. That's why Jesus denounced the people of Chorazin and Bethsaida (Matt 11:21—towns along the Sea of Galilee where Jesus preached). And tough for anyone in any town that would "not welcome you or listen to your words," he told his disciples, because "it will be more bearable for Sodom and Gomorrah on the day of judgment than for that town" (Matt 10:14–15 NIV). In *ten* separate verses in the gospels, Jesus drives home the point that judgment covers a period of time and will involve some hearty discipline (and, apparently, shaming).

Jesus declared that the men of Nineveh, the capital of Assyria, who were horrifically evil in God's eyes (Nah 2:13), "will rise up in the judgment with this generation and condemn it, because they repented at the preaching of Jonah; and indeed a greater than Jonah is here" (Matt 12:41 NKJV). So, too, those from the Baal-worshipping cities of Tyre and Sidon (home to the wicked queen Jezebel—1 Kgs 16:31) will find the period of the judgment "more tolerable" than those who heard Jesus but rejected him (Luke 10:14 NKJV).

Why will all these wicked people "fare better"? Because those towns witnessed the miracles Jesus empowered his disciples to perform in his name, and those towns refused to believe that he was the promised Messiah.

In the future, those inhabitants will wake up in the new earth and, to their shock, they will find that the man they rejected is now the ruling, powerful King of Kings. And if they don't humble themselves, repent, and get with the program, they're going to have a hard row to hoe. This isn't a picture of perfect peace and harmony. We're told in Revelation that, even after a thousand years of seeing the kind of loving, gracious, and just king Jesus will be, a third of the earth will turn against Christ and side with the temporarily released devil at the end of the reign of Christ. No wonder God has arranged to have a government set up with rulers and judges serving alongside Jesus. There's going to be a lot of work to be done in people's hearts during this time.

When "the end comes," after the devil, his demons, and all their followers are destroyed, Christ will turn the kingdom over to God, his Father, and subject himself to God's sovereignty (1 Cor 15:25), so God will finally and ultimately be "all in all" (verse 28).

Different Generations Living Together

I'd like to point out something that's been bothering me for decades. It's not often that some event or words of Jesus are repeated in the gospels. I've heard church pastors and theologians say that when something is repeated three times (for emphasis), it means we need to pay particular attention.

The Dead Who "Do Not Come to Life" until the End

For instance, Jesus's baptism at the Jordan River is recounted in three of the gospels. It was an important event in Jesus's life. What's commonly called "The Lord's Prayer" is recorded in only two gospels, yet it's a benchmark of Christianity.

But this pronouncement about who will rise in the resurrection, how they will fare, and who will be there is found in *ten* passages. Ten times Jesus elucidates the situation in which those resurrected—both "righteous and unrighteous"—will not be immediately sent off to judgment but will all be living on the earth together. People from ancient Assyria who lived eight centuries before Christ will be making some harsh remarks to those who had lived hundreds of years later in Israel, during the time Jesus preached. The queen of Sheba, who visited Solomon when he was king over Israel, will "rise up" and condemn these resurrected Israelites of Jesus's day who refused to listen to him—she lived more than nine hundred years before these folks she's going to give a mouthful to (Matt 12:42; Luke 11:31).

Yet . . . in the decades that I have read and listened to Bible instruction through books, sermons, podcasts, and Bible apps, I have not once—never—heard any discussion of these ten passages. I find that suspect. Ten whole passages that prove the judgment will be on earth, involve numerous generations, involve people from Sodom and Gomorrah and the cities that rejected Jesus, all in discussion about the rulership and authority of Christ. Can you picture some lowlife from Sodom chastising a disbeliever who had once seen in person the miracles Jesus performed and scoffed? Think about the thief that hung alongside Jesus, who berated his fellow criminal in defense of Jesus's divine authority? No doubt that discussion will continue in paradise, with the newly converted thief, now resurrected into Jesus's kingdom along with his pal, saying, "I told you so . . ." (Luke 23:39–43).

All musings aside, this shines a light on a serious problem, and this is why I urge you to prayerfully study God's Word and do your homework. The entire Word of God is beneficial for teaching and setting things straight, I noted at the start of this book. But if teachers of the Bible ignore whole sections of the Scriptures, and notably the gospels, that can spell danger because it provides an incomplete patchwork picture of salvation.

CHAPTER 17

The Final Judgment and the Sets of Books

IN REVELATION WE LEARN there are two sets of books that are opened. No, not like how crooks keep two sets of books—one accurate and the other falsified. At the final judgment we see the Lamb's Book of Life (Rev 21:27), but there are other books that are opened at the final judgment, and "the dead were judged out of those things which were written in the books, according to their works" (Rev 20:12 NASB).

As with most of Revelation, this passage harkens to one in the Old Testament, in this case Daniel chapter 7, which details the events of God's judgment. Daniel, in his dreams, sees "one like a son of man, and he came to the Ancient of Days and was presented before him. And to him was given dominion and glory and a kingdom, that all peoples, nations, and languages should serve him," then notes this kingdom will not pass away or be destroyed, as were the other kingdoms in Daniel's vision (verses 13–14 ESV).

In verses 9–10, we read:

> As I looked,
> thrones were placed,
> and the Ancient of Days took his seat;
> his clothing was white as snow,
> and the hair of his head like pure wool;
> his throne was fiery flames;
> its wheels were burning fire.
> A stream of fire issued
> and came out from before him;
> a thousand thousands served him,

and ten thousand times ten thousand stood before him;
the court sat in judgment,
and the books were opened.

We're told in Revelation chapter 20 that the dead are judged according to their deeds. Let's pause here and review what we already know to be fact in the Bible. When a person dies, they have paid the full price for their sin, for the wages of sin is death. Even though "God shall bring every work into judgment, with every secret thing, whether it be good, or whether it be evil" (Eccl 12:14 KJV), because of Jesus's sacrifice, "their sins and their lawless deeds I will remember no more" (Heb 10:17 NKJV). That means no one would *ever* be resurrected and then judged on their *prior* deeds done before they died. Let me repeat this.

A Clean Slate for Everyone

Anyone resurrected has a clean slate. While that may sound wrong, how can it be? If you are appointed to die once, and the payment you make for being a sinner is dying, you can't be charged and made to pay *again* for a debt you already paid. Everyone who dies has paid the price. The Bible clearly states this. Every person would be dead forever if Jesus hadn't picked up the tab and paid the debt for us. That gave us the opportunity for a 2.0 reboot.

Now, Jesus came so that people could have life—not just a short sin-filled life but life in abundance (John 10:10). The life Jesus gives is eternal life that will spring up from inside the believer—just as Adam and Eve had but forfeited. That's why they were put out of the garden, so they couldn't eat of the tree of life.

No, a literal tree does not grant endless life to the eater. Their access to the garden symbolized their obedience to God and the condition upon which they could keep on living. If they had sinned and eaten from the tree of the knowledge of good and bad eight hundred years after being created, they would still have been kicked out of the garden and prevented from eating from "the tree of life." Remember: Adam and Eve were allowed to eat from every tree in the garden except one—that forbidden "knowledge" tree. That means they had permission to eat from the tree of life at any time. Perhaps they did. Maybe it wasn't anything special in the way of tasty fruit. The tree wasn't surrounded by a locked barbed-wire fence so the first couple couldn't eat from it. That's how we know the tree is symbolic (see Rev 2:7). Being in the garden, having freedom of choice, of movement, free from pain and death, was a privilege represented by that tree of life situated in the center of the garden. When Adam and Eve sinned, they lost their garden pass. But I digress. Let's get back to judgment.

If "the dead, great and small, standing before the throne," where the books are opened, are to be "judged according to their works" (Rev 20:12), what works would those be? Now that we understand there will be nations and kingdoms on the earth under Christ's rule—those nations that will have to learn war no more and whom Christ will shepherd "with an iron rod" (Ps 2:9)—we can assume that all those resurrected people, including the disbelievers of Jesus's day and the inhabitants of Sodom, are not perfect, incorruptible, or sinless during this thousand years. They haven't "come to life yet," nor have they been raised up incorruptible in the manner Paul explains in 1 Corinthians chapter 15. They have some "learning" to do.

What does this mean? That while those who are asleep in Christ are raised first and are promised to be raised up incorruptible—right from the start—not subject to the second death, that's *not* the case for unbelievers.

Unbelievers Are Not Raised Incorruptible

Now, that paints an interesting situation—a planet filled with a combination of immortal, incorruptible humans and nations populated with imperfect, still sinful humans who don't "come to life" or get granted immortality until the final judgment at the end of Christ's reign (if they qualify). This also adds weight and reason to the declaration that the faithful will rule as kings and priests with Jesus for the whole thousand years. The King of Kings says, "To the one who is victorious, I will give the right to sit with me on my throne, just as I was victorious and sat down with my Father on his throne" (Rev 3:21 NIV. See also Rev 2:25–27; 5:10; 20:6). The apostle Paul puts it plainly: "Do do you not know that the saints will judge the world?" (1 Cor 6:2 ESV). It's a whole lot easier to rule if you are sinless and incorruptible than if sin still rules in your body. And let me remind you that many teach that these rulers are going to be in heaven with Jesus as spirit beings, even though the Bible plainly states Christ and they will rule on earth. There is no one to rule over in heaven. God already rules there.

And if you believe all unbelievers or wicked people will be resurrected and instantly sent off into punishment (to suffer torment forever in some immortal spirit body), why the need for priests—ever considered that? Priests intercede between God and mankind. Jesus is the high priest and the only mediator between God and humans for salvation (1 Tim 2:5). But obviously a function of the kingdom over the thousand years of Christ's rule will include priestly activities—some form of intercession and judging of those resurrected—similar to the function of the judges God had appointed back in Israel, before the people insisted on a king. Jesus said to his apostles in Matthew 19:28 (ESV): "Truly, I say to you, in the new world, when the Son of Man will sit on his glorious throne, you who have followed me will also sit on twelve thrones, judging the twelve tribes of Israel."

After these ten centuries of living on earth under Christ's government, those who hadn't been imbued with incorruptibility at the start of the millennium are then brought before the throne, where all their works are recorded in these books. What works? Well, if the works they did *before* they died had been paid off *in full* by their deaths, then it must be the works they've done under kingdom rule *during the millennium*.

So, I will leave this for you to dig further into. There are many things about the future that are "sealed up until the time of the end" (Dan 12:4) and other things just not explained in the Bible at all—because, clearly, God did not feel it necessary we know some things until "we get there."

One thing we can be assured of—God is just and righteous. He will punish evil and disobedience, but he is merciful. Allowing every person who has ever lived an opportunity to know Jesus and grow in love and gratitude for him, his sacrifice, and his righteous rulership—for a thousand years—is an amazing act of grace and something wholly in keeping with the character of God, one of the three C's of scriptural accuracy.

In 1 Corinthians 15:48–49 (NIV) we read: "As was the earthly man, so are those who are of the earth; and as is the heavenly man, so also are those who are of heaven [partakers, beneficiaries, whose names are enrolled in heaven—Heb 12:23]. And just as we have borne the image of the earthly man, so shall we bear the image of the heavenly man." (Pay attention to that wording. It speaks of just one heavenly man, not countless heavenly men. This harmonizes with all the Scriptures that state Jesus is the only man—the only human—who has ever gone to heaven.)

It's when "the perishable has been clothed with the imperishable, and the mortal with immortality, then the saying that is written will come true: Death has been swallowed up in victory" (verse 54). Paul is speaking specifically about believers and their future bodies. All these things are not given a specific time period in relation to the judgment at the end of the thousand years, but it might be assumed that for believers this transformation will be immediate, upon resurrection into the kingdom as the firstfruits raised from the dead because those in Christ are promised to be raised in and like him. But not so with those *not* in Christ.

The Lamb's Book of Life

There is another interesting, related reference to books that God keeps:

> Then those who feared the Lord talked with each other, and the Lord listened and heard. A scroll of remembrance was written in his presence concerning those who feared the Lord and honored his name. "On the day when I act," says the Lord Almighty, "they will be my treasured possession. I will spare them, just as a father has compassion and spares his son who serves him." (Mal 3:16–17 NIV)

Jesus told his followers in Luke 10:20: "Nevertheless do not rejoice in this, that the spirits are subject to you, but rejoice that your names are recorded in heaven." God has been jotting down names. And everyone who accepts Christ has their name added to the list in the Book of Life. However, Jesus warned that a person's name could be removed from his Book of Life: "The one who conquers will be clothed thus in white garments, and I will never blot his name out of the book of life. I will confess his name before my Father and before his angels" (Rev 3:5 ESV). By Jesus saying this, he indicates that those who do *not* conquer will run the risk of having their name blotted out. And not only Moses but God himself spoke about "blotting" people's names from his book (Exod 32:31–33). Another truth in Scripture that shoots down the common but erroneous "once saved, always saved" doctrine.

The Lamb's Book of Life is different from the books that are opened before the white throne at Judgment Day at the end of the thousand years. The Book of Life has the names of everyone who will be granted immortality (and maybe also the names of those faithful who have, before that time, already been granted it). That's the list of names. Certainly those who follow the devil after his short release at the end of the millennium do not have their names in that book. Or, if they do, out comes the eraser. The other books list all the *works* resurrected people have done during their trial period. It's fascinating to see how many references in the Scriptures there are to these important books (Phil 4:3; Ps 69:27–28; Rev 21:27—to note a few).

Let me interject a thought about the "sheep and goats" parable in Matthew 25. We have to keep in mind the very clear and simple timeline regarding judgment. When Jesus returns from heaven and separates people into two camps—the sheep who did good to "the least of these, my brothers" with a promise of eternal life and the goats who failed to do the requisite "good" and are told they will go into the lake of fire with the devil and his hordes—he isn't going to execute that judgment immediately. If he did, that would mean he is going to judge only the people who are alive on earth when he comes. What about the billions of people who lived and died since the creation of humankind? It makes no sense to believe Jesus would only judge a portion of all who lived and ignore the rest.

It's important to adjust your thinking about "judgment" to a process over time, not a singular pronouncement. Yes, at the end of the judgment period, there will be that definitive moment of pronouncement, but that isn't the whole of "judgment." That winnowing of the sheep and goats takes place over the thousand years, with people from every moment of time past brought back to life to be instructed in God's ways. At some point, the earth will be filled with the knowledge of the Lord as the waters cover the seas (Hab 2:14), because, by "the end," every knee will bow and every tongue will confess that Jesus is Lord (Phil 2:10–11; cf. Rom 14:11).

The Threshold for Passing from Death to Life

The apostle John writes, "We know that we have passed from death to life, because we love the brethren. He who does not love his brother abides in death. Whoever hates his brother is a murderer, and you know that no murderer has eternal life abiding in him" (1 John 3:14-15 NKJV). There is a threshold under which we pass from death to life. Jesus is the way and the life, and when we believe in him, we are given not just the privilege, John says, but *the right* to become children of God, adopted into his family, heirs of the promise (John 1:12; Rom 8:17). What promise? Eternal life and immortality. (And note, here, how John contrasts the two possible options: death and life. Not life with Jesus vs. endless life in a tormented state.)

Paul says in Romans 8:29–30 (NKJV): "For whom He foreknew, He also predestined to be conformed to the image of his Son, that He might be the firstborn among many brethren. Moreover whom He predestined, these He also called; whom He called, these He also justified; and whom He justified, these He also glorified." So it stands to reason that believers' names are already written in the Lamb's Book of Life—maybe even from the beginning of the creation of the world. The writer of Hebrews in chapter 12 verse 23 also refers to those "enrolled" (ESV) or "registered" (NKJV) in heaven or have "names written in heaven" (NLT).

But not just *their* names. What would be the point of resurrecting everyone who ever lived to be subjects of the kingdom for a thousand years and not give them the possibility of getting into the book? Seems kind of futile to bring them back to life, only to tell them there's an expiration date stamped on their foreheads—no exceptions. Remember, we're told many of these folks "come to life" or "come into life" at the end of that "probation period."

Is that fair? Well, they're not being judged according to the defunct Mosaic Law, which was impossible to keep—all pointing to the need of Jesus's perfect sacrifice as the last Adam, which allows Jesus to become their new "Everlasting Father" (Isa 9:6–7). Instead, they're going to be judged by what they do under perfect divine rule, with perfect knowledge of the truth—no deception or veil or obscurity or demonic misinformation. During the kingdom reign not only will instruction pour from the throne, we're told that no one will have to learn who God is because "they shall all know him, from the least to the greatest" and the knowledge of God and of Christ will fill the earth as "the waters cover the very seas."

Can you imagine what a wholly different place the earth will be with 100 percent accurate knowledge of the truth and a righteous king ruling on the throne over all people? Now, should anyone choose to disobey or decide they don't want to "get with the program," they can't use the excuse that they didn't know what was good or bad or didn't understand what's expected of them from God. They can't complain they were confused or misled or ignorant.

I wouldn't expect anything less from a fair and just God than this—to give everyone an informed and gracious opportunity to live and experience life in abundance under Jesus's rule. I think of all the millions of people who never got a chance at any kind of decent life—those who died of starvation, those enslaved, those without any hope or knowledge of God in the world, those who died at birth or in early childhood. How incredible this time will be—a time when everyone will build their own houses and live in them

The Final Judgment and the Sets of Books

instead of build houses for someone else and have to sleep on a cold street corner (Isa 65:21). Everyone will sit, each under their own vine and fig tree, with nothing to make them afraid (Mic 4:4) as the earth is restored to the original perfect state that God intended it would be. Each will enjoy equity, healing (a process—see Rev 22:2), and equal opportunity to know and love Jesus. In the end, everyone will have the same facts to help them choose whether or not to accept his authority. Jesus's job for that one-thousand-year judgment period is to bring all things together in heaven and earth under God—and by subsequently turning over the kingdom to God, Christ then submits himself to his Father, God (1 Cor 15:24).

Anyone can have their name written in the Book of Life—even if they never knew of or accepted Jesus when they were previously alive. By showing "good works" in faithfulness to Christ during this kingdom rule, they can choose life. But, they can also have their name erased. If one's name is not in the Book of Life, it merely means life—in any form—will not be made available to them (see Rev 17:8). The opposite of life is nonexistence. You are either alive or you are not. You either "come to life"—get gifted with immortality through belief and obedience to Christ—or you do not come to life. It's truly simple, just, and consistent with all Scripture.

How much more believable is this biblically based picture of judgment compared to one in which God resurrects all those who didn't know or accept Jesus (the majority of humankind) at the very *end* of the thousand-year rule, reads their judgment from his books based on their past sins (of which they already paid the price through their death), and tosses them into a torturous fire to suffer and scream in agony for eternity? To me, this gruesome picture of God is an affront to God's character—and I hope you see that too. A God who loved the world so much that he gave his Son would never be so unjust as to punish people like this. And that should make us love him all the more!

CHAPTER 18

One Mind and One Voice

THE APOSTLE PAUL, IN closing his letter to the believers in Rome, penned these words:

> Everything that was written in the past was written to teach us, so that through the endurance taught in the Scriptures and the encouragement they provide we might have hope. May the God who gives endurance and encouragement give you the same attitude of mind toward each other that Christ Jesus had, so that with one mind and one voice you may glorify the God and Father of our Lord Jesus Christ. (Rom 15:4–6 NIV)

All we have to do is look at the history of the church, from the first century until now, to see how believers have failed in achieving the unity of mind and voice Paul urged. Jesus prayed to his Father expressing his desire that his followers "be one" just as he himself was one with the Father (John 17:21). That seems such a tall order—an unanswered prayer. And here, with these insights into death, hell, resurrection, and judgment, an attempt to pull away from the traditional teachings of Christianity portends even more division.

What's a believer to do—when faced with teachings that the Bible, in its entirety, consistently disproves? Do we just throw up our hands and say that in the end it doesn't matter? That truth is a matter of interpretation? That keeping peace and aiming for unity is worth the cost of compromise and silence? I leave that up to you to wrestle with. Arguments over doctrine rarely lead to unity—in fact, the opposite.

Will a person lose salvation if they don't have every teaching nailed down perfectly in alignment with the Scriptures? No. Jesus said it is *belief* in him that leads to eternal life. Belief and obedience. But knowledge shouldn't be ignored. "And this is the way to have eternal life—to know you, the only true God, and Jesus Christ, the one you sent to earth" (John 17:3 NLT). Our aim as we grow in our faith is to know God and Christ more deeply, more accurately, more intimately with each day's passing. Everyone is in a different stage in their journey to become a mature Christian, but we are urged to move beyond the basics and the "milk" of the Word (see 1 Cor 3:2). The writer of Hebrews didn't mince words: "We have much to say about [Jesus], but it is hard to make it clear to you because you no longer try to understand. In fact, though by this time you ought to be teachers, you need someone to teach you the elementary truths of God's word all over again. You need milk, not solid food!" (Heb 5:11–12 NIV). We shouldn't shy away from challenging the things we hear, digging into the Scriptures to confirm or discount any teaching, and yet keep humble—that thirsty pilgrim in the wilderness looking for a sip of water.

We shouldn't care what others think about us. Our standing, our reputation, our position shouldn't be more important than truth. Recall what Pastor Gregory Stump said: "I have often faced alienation and marginalization from peers who have vehemently disagreed with me along with the ongoing potential of losing my job over the view of hell that I held." It takes courage to stand up for truth. The annals of history are filled with the names of Christian leaders who were murdered for defying the current doctrine of their time. But we also are commanded to seek unity of mind and heart with our fellow believers. However, in the end, what matters above all is our relationship with our heavenly Father.

The most important reason we need to understand, accept, and believe this truth about judgment and the fate of those who do not accept God's plan of salvation is God's character. At the start of this book, I mentioned how it is God's deep desire that his human creation comes to know and love him, and that we are urged to have a healthy fear of God—one of utter awe, respect, and humility.

But we cannot truly love our Creator if we believe he finds it just and righteous to inflict horrific pain upon his creatures. If we look at the times in the Bible when God meted out destruction directly upon individuals or groups, such as the unfaithful Israelites in the wilderness or various armies attacking his people, he or an appointed angel had them destroyed quickly, if not instantly. You will never find any instance of God prolonging suffering and torturing any individual, no matter how evil. Yes, God has and will punish and destroy evildoers. But he has told us how much he detested those who made a practice of burning their children in fire as a sacrifice to false gods. Something that horrific and egregious never came into his heart. In other words, he would never consider doing such a terrible thing.

How important is it to you that other believers have a true understanding of God's nature regarding judgment, hell, and resurrection? That's for you to determine, and the Bible reminds us there is a time to speak and a time to refrain from speaking (Eccl 3:7). May we all ask God to give us wisdom and discernment so we can speak the truth yet cultivate peace and unity among our fellow believers.

The Glorious Future Awaiting Us

There's a lot we don't know about the future. The Bible has been given to us to understand God, and whatever it doesn't address, God clearly didn't feel it important to tell us. Will we someday travel to the stars? When the earth is full, will humans and animals stop reproducing (since God's directive was "Fill the earth and subdue it")?

I like to imagine God is going to give us all a giant-size bucket of popcorn and usher us into the coolest 3D surround-sound theater to watch the entire story of history, from the creation of the universe and this planet to all the events over the last six thousand years. How amazing would it be to watch actual footage of Jesus's time on earth? Could we select a person, place, and time in history and watch exactly what transpired? Will there be a video/holographic library in which we can learn the truth of every moment of the past? Who knows? I'd sure love to watch God create the cosmos. I'd want a front-row seat.

We're told in Scripture that we will be made in the likeness of Jesus, the one from heaven, but what that body will be like, we don't know. We do know, though, it will be perfect, sinless, incorruptible. Our bodies will be like Jesus's—he ate and drank and walked after he was resurrected (Luke 24:40–43). He promised he would eat food and drink wine with us in his kingdom (Matt 26:29). He had flesh—he had Thomas touch his scars (which he perhaps manifested to convince doubting Thomas that he was really the raised Christ—John 20:27). Jesus walked on water and made it possible for Peter to join him in that physics-defying behavior. Are we going to be able to do that? (Matt 14:25–30). To manipulate matter and electromagnetism?

The angels have the ability to take on human form; will we have some special powers in these new immortal, incorruptible bodies?

Who knows what our true earthly perfect human bodies will be able to do. We'll have to wait and see. But I hope you are excited for that day, when you and everyone on earth will "know the Lord, from the least to the great," and everyone will sit under his own vine and fig tree, and no one will make them tremble.

There are so many promises of eternal life here on earth, and, honestly, why would anyone want to go live as a spirit or angel in heaven when Jesus will be down here? I don't know about you, but I want to be here with him, in his kingdom, on earth, praising him for eternity, just as one of my favorite Scriptures declares: "You will show me the way of life, granting me the joy of your presence and the pleasures of living with you forever" (Ps 16:11 NLT). Can I get an amen?

Bibliography

Anonymous. *The Cambridge Bible for Schools and Colleges*. Vol. 51, Sydney, Australia: Wentworth, 2019.
Bacchiocchi, Samuele, and Clark Pinnock. *Immortality or Resurrection? A Biblical Study on Human Nature and Destiny*. Berrien Springs, MI: Biblical Perspectives, 1997.
Benson, Joseph. *Benson Commentary*. https://biblehub.com/commentaries/benson/romans/13.htm.
Bowles, Ralph G. "Does Revelation 14:11 Teach Eternal Torment? Examining a Proof-text on Hell." *The Evangelical Quarterly* 73:1 (2001) 32–33. https://biblicalstudies.org.uk/pdf/eq/2001-1_021.pdf.
"Commentary on Hebrews 3." "Cambridge Greek Testament for Schools and Colleges." https://www.studylight.org/commentaries/eng/cgt/hebrews-3.html. 1896.
Cooper, John W. *Body, Soul, and Life Everlasting: Biblical Anthropology and the Monism-Dualism Debate*. Grand Rapids, MI: Wm. B. Eerdmans, 2000.
Crim, Keith, and George Buttrick. *The Interpreter's Dictionary of the Bible*. Nashville, TN: Abingdon, 1981.
Date, Christopher, et al. *Rethinking Hell: Readings in Evangelical Conditionalism*, xi–xii. Eugene, OR: Cascade, 2014.
Davis, R. Magnusson. "Heaven, Sheol, and Gehenna: What Happened to Heaven and Hell?" https://newmatthewbible.org/WhateverHappenedtoHell.pdf.
Edwards, David L., and John Stott. *Evangelical Essentials: A Liberal-Evangelical Dialogue*, 314. London: Hodder & Stoughton, 1988.
Fudge, Edward William. *The Fire That Consumes: A Biblical and Historical Study of the Doctrine of Final Punishment. 3rd Edition, Fully Updated, Revised and Expanded*. 3rd ed., Eugene OR: Cascade, 2011.
Gesenius, Wilhelm. *Genenius's Hebrew and Chaldee Lexicon to the Old Testament Scriptures*. Andesite, 2015.
Guzik, David. "Hebrew 3—Jesus, Superior to Moses." *Enduring Word*. https://enduringword.com/bible-commentary/hebrews-3/.
Hanson, J. W. *Bible Threatenings Explained*. Boston, MA: Universalist, 1885.
Henry, Matthew. *Matthew Henry's Commentary*. https://biblehub.com/commentaries/mhc/romans/13.htm.
Hurt, Bruce. "Hebrews 3:1–4 Commentary." *Precept Austin*. https://www.preceptaustin.org/hebrews.
Jeremiah, David. *Answers to Your Questions about Heaven*. Carol Stream, IL: Tyndale, 2015.

Bibliography

The Jewish Encyclopedia: Philipson-Samoscz. United Kingdom: Funk & Wagnalls, 1909.

Kaiser, Walter C. Jr. *Recovering the Unity of the Bible: One Continuous Story, Plan, and Purpose*. Grand Rapids, MI: Zondervan, 2009.

Keller, Edmund B. "Hebrew Thoughts on Immortality and Resurrection." *International Journal for Philosophy of Religion* 5, no. 1 (1974) 16-44. Accessed January 21, 2021. http://www.jstor.org/stable/40021203.

"Lecture—Edward Fudge—The Fire That Consumes: A Biblical and Historical Study of Hell." *YouTube*, uploaded by Lanier Theological Library, 24 Oct. 2011, www.youtube.com/watch?v=oHUPpmbTOV4.

Merriam-Webster and Inc. *Merriam-Webster's Collegiate Dictionary, 11th Edition, Jacketed Hardcover, Indexed, 2020 Copyright*. 11th ed., Springfield, MA, G. & C. Merriam Co., 2019.

Micou, Richard Wilde. *Basic Ideas in Religion: Or Apologetic Theism (Classic Reprint)*. London: Forgotten, 2018.

Morey, Robert. *Death and the Afterlife*. Underlining, Bloomington, MN: Bethany House, 1984.

Morris, Leon. "The Dreadful Harvest." *Christianity Today*. May 1991. https://www.christianitytoday.com/ct/1991/may-27/dreadful-harvest.html.

"The Neshama—Breath or Soul?" *The Four Questions of Judaism*. http://fourquestionsofjudaism.com/5663998322147328.

"Revelation 6:9." *Bible Study Tools*. https://www.biblestudytools.com/commentaries/revelation/revelation-6/revelation-6-9.html.

Russell, Bertrand. *The Basic Writings of Bertrand Russell, 1903-1959*. Edited by Lester Denonn and Robert Egner, New York, NY: Simon and Schuster, 1961.

"The Second Coming of Christ." *Moody Bible Institute*. https://www.moodybible.org/beliefs/positional-statements/second-coming/.

Strong, James. *The New Strong's Expanded Exhaustive Concordance of the Bible*. Expanded, Nashville, TN: Thomas Nelson, 2010.

Thayer, John. *The New Thayer's Greek-English Lexicon of the New Testament*. Peabody, MA: Hendrickson, 1988.

Thornbury, Gregory, and Paul House, editors. *Who Will Be Saved?: Defending the Biblical Understanding of God, Salvation, and Evangelism*. Wheaton, IL: Crossway, 2000.

Thriepland, L. J. "Does 2 Corinthians 5–8 Teach That Believers Will Go to Heaven When They Die?' *Follow in Truth*. https://www.followintruth.com/does-2-corinthians-5-8-teach-that-believers-will-go-to-heaven-when-they-die.

"Titus' Siege of Jerusalem - Livius." *Livius.Org*, Oct. 2020, www.livius.org/articles/concept/roman-jewish-wars/roman-jewish-wars-4.

Vu, Michelle A., "Interview: Scholar Edward Fudge on Alternate Third View of Hell." *The Christian Post*, June 2011. https://www.christianpost.com/news/interview-scholar-edward-fudge-on-alternative-third-view-of-hell.html.

"What Is the Rapture?" *Crossway*, Oct. 2018. https://www.crossway.org/articles/what-is-the-rapture-1-thessalonians-4/.

Index

OLD TESTAMENT

Genesis
	29
1	28
1:1	8
2:7	32
2:7 ESV	26
2:17	26
3:4	27
3:8 NIV	98
3:19	17
3:19 ESV	27
3:22–23	28
3:24	28
4:10	73
5:5	135
5:24	35, 65
5:24 NLT	65
9:4 ESV	32
25:8	32
28:16	90
35:2	46
35:29	32
37:35 ESV	38
49:29	32

Exodus
12:12	46
16:10	101
32:31–33	148
33:7–11	98
33:9	101
40:15	85

Leviticus
4:7	73
16	112
19:31	46
20:6, 27	45
20:27	45
24:8	85
26:3–13	134
26:14–17	134
26:18 NKJV	134
26:19–20	134

Numbers
11:25	101
12:5	101
16:31–33 ESV	38
19:1	28

Deuteronomy
4:24	87
12:31 ESV	14
30:19	126
31:16	91

Judges
4:18	103
11:31, 34	103
11:34	103
19:3	103

Index

1 Samuel
13:10	103
28:3–20 NKJV	44–45
28:19	46
30:11–12 KJV	33

2 Samuel
7:12	91

1 Kings
1:21	39
2:10 ESV	91
8:10	101
8:13	85
11:43	39
16:31	142

2 Kings
2:11 ESV	66
2:15–18	66
16:3	78
18:10	135
23:10	78

1 Chronicles
10:6	45
10:13–14	45

2 Chronicles
2:6 ESV	98
21:12	66

Nehemiah
2:1–8	135

Job
3:11, 13, 17	37
3:13	37
3:17	37
10:9	27
10:21	39
11:7–9	51
14:13	36
16:9	126
18:15	82
19:25–27	39
22:14	101
26:5	42
26:6 KJV	38
27:3	32
33:4 NKJV	32
34:14–15 KJV	33
38:17 KJV	51

Psalms
1:4	122
2:7–9	121
2:9	122, 146
2:9 NIV	137
4:8 ESV	90
9:7–8	128
16:10	36
16:11	15
16:11 NLT	155
18:11	101
35:16	126
37	93
37:2	122
37:10	123, 126
37:11	102
37:34	126
56:4	83
58:7	122
58:8	122
58:10	126
68:2	122
69:27–28	149
78:2	53
83:13	122
88:3–4 NIV	38
88:10	42
88:10–11 NIV	38–39
90:3 NIV	17
91:8 NIV	126
92:6–7 NIV	35, 89
94:17 NIV	39
103:14	27
110:5–6	122
112:10	126

Index

112:10 KJV	76	26:13, 19	42
115:16	98	26:14	43
115:16 NLT	18	26:19	42
115:17	39	26:19 NIV	18
116:15 NIV	104	30:31–33	78
121:4–6	90	30:33	82
139:7–8 KJV	38	34:9–10 KJV	81
139:7–10	86	34:10	82, 88
		37:36	78, 83

Proverbs

2:18	42	42:25	112
9:18	42	55:11	104
15:11	38	55:12	38
19:15	90	57:2 NIV	37
20:13	90	65:17	132
21:16	42	65:21	151
24:33–34	90	65:25	132
27:20	38	66:1	98
		66:15–16 ESV	83
		66:23–24	83
		66:24	78

Ecclesiastes

1:4	104		
1:4 ESV	62	## Jeremiah	
1:4 KJV	62	4:4	88
3:7	154	7:20	88
9:2	39	7:32–33 ESV	78
9:5–6 ESV	39	21:12	88
9:6	126	25:27	85
9:10	39	29:11	137
12	31	29:13	3
12:7 ESV	33	31:31	9
12:7 NKJV	32	31:34	102
12:14 KJV	145	48:4, 42, 47	85
		48:42	85
		48:47	85
		49:6	85
		49:39	85

Isaiah

1:31	82		
2:2–4 NIV	88	## Lamentations	
5:11	131	2:16	126
8:19	18		
9:6	46	## Ezekiel	
9:6–7	115	3:11 ESV	1
9:7 ESV	150	4:4	123
9:7 NIV	140	4:4–8	134
11:9	102	18:4	134
14:3–11 NKJV	102		17, 27
14:9	40–41		
	42, 43		

Index

Ezekiel (*continued*)

20	88
20:47–48	88
31:2	41
31:3–9	41
31:10–14	41
31:15–18 NIV	41–42
32:27	42
33:11	14
37:9 NKJV	32
38:22	82

Daniel

2:44	137
7:9–10	144–145
7:13–14 ESV	144
7:13–14 KJV	60
8:18	90
9:25–26	134
12:2	27
12:2 NIV	90, 129
12:4	5, 147
12:13	45
12:13 NIV	60

Hosea

13:3 KJV	123
13:14	115

Amos

5:6	88
9:2 ESV	38
9:2–3	51

Micah

4:4	151

Nahum

2:13	142

Habakkuk

1:13	112
2:14	102, 149

Zephaniah

1:4	76
1:14–15, 18 NKJV	75
1:15, 18	126
1:18	126
2:9	85

Malachi

	29
3:16–17 NIV	148
4:1 NIV	87
4:2	6
4:3 NKJV	87
4:5 ESV	48

NEW TESTAMENT

Matthew

1:24	91
3:11–12 NKJV	87
5	79
5:5	101, 126
5:8	137
5:22, 29–30	79
5:29–30	79
6:33 NKJV	110
7:13–14	86
8:11–12 NRSV	56
10:14–15 NIV	142
10:15	18
10:28	80
11:20	51
11:21	141
11:23 ESV	51
11:24	18
11:29	30
12:18	30
12:32 NIV	116
12:41 NKJV	142
12:42	143
13:13–14 NKJV	54
13:19	105
13:30–40	13
13:34–35 NIV	53

Index

13:48	13
14:25–30	154
15:13	13
16:18	51
16:26 KJV	29
16:28	47
17:1–13 ESV	47–48
17:21–23 NIV	47
18	87
18:9	80
19:28 ESV	147
21:40 NKJV	123
21:43–44	123
22	135
22:23–31	135
22:28 NKJV	136
22:29–32	136
23:15	80
23:26	110
23:33	85, 88
24:30	101
24:34	88
24:37–39 NKJV	94
24:38–31 NIV	102
24:40–42	94
24:51	123
25	102, 103, 149
25:5	90
25:6	85, 103
25:31	137
25:31–46	118, 129
25:41–46	84
25:46	86
26:29	6, 154
26:64	101
27:46 ESV	112
27:52	91

Mark

7:24–30	55
9	87
9:1 NIV	47
9:43	80
9:45	80
9:47	80
10:37	109
10:37 NLT	109
10:38–39 NIV	109
10:45 KJV	30
12:18–27	135
12:27 NLT	101
13:26	101
14:58 ESV	71

Luke

8:52	91
8:55 KJV	33
9:22	47
9:32	91
10:14 NKJV	142
10:16	123
10:20	148
11:31	143
12:5	84
13:2–3	123
13:3	122
13:4–5	123
13:7	13
13:28–29	59
15:24, 32	139
15:32	139
16:1–13	55
16:14	55
16:19–31	53
16:23	55
17:21	110
17:27	123
17:29	123
17:34–36	126
18:30	85
19:14, 27	123
19:27	123
20:27–40	135
20:38 NKJV	136
20:38 NLT	100–101
22:29–30 KJV	59
22:31	47
22:45	91
23:39–43	143
23:42–43	52
23:46 KJV	32
24:40–43	154
24:44 NIV	48

Index

John

1:1–3	8
1:12	149
1:12 ESV	115
1:14	97
3:5–6 NIV	67
3:13	64, 132
3:16 KJV	12
4:13–14 NKJV	29
4:14	107
4:24	20
5:22	128
5:24 NKJV	141
5:25–29	133
5:28 NLT	18
6:39–40, 54	133
6:40 NIV	18
6:54	133
6:63 NKJV	34
7:16, 18	67
7:18	67
8:21	16
8:24	91
8:32	21
10:10	145
10:28	105
10:28 NKJV	101
10:29	105
11:11	58, 91
11:13	91
11:25–26 ESV	92
13:23	55
13:33 NLT	108
13:36 NLT	108
14:2	101
14:3	59
14:6	10, 34
15:6	13, 89
16:13	5
17:3 NLT	153
17:21	152
20:17 NIV	52
20:27	154

Acts

	101
1:11	101
2:27	36
2:34	60
2:41–43	29
4:12 NIV	115
7:1–5	60
7:14	29
7:51 NIV	116
7:53	116
7:54 NASB	126
7:60	91
9:12	49
10	61
10:3, 17, 19	49
10:17	49
10:19	49
10:41	129
10:43 NIV	115
12:9	49
16:9	49
16:30–31 NIV	116
17	61
17:27	3
17:31	57, 72, 135
17:31 NIV	128
20:9	91
22:3	61
24:15	18
24:25	61
26:22–23 ESV	108
28	103
28:15	103

Romans

2:5–9	53
2:5–9 ESV	75
2:5–11 NIV	128
2:6 NKJV	125
2:7 ESV	29
2:7–9 ESV	125
2:9	29
2:12	61
3:2	6, 55
4:13	60
5:8 KJV	9
5:12	28
5:12–21	30

Index

6:3–4 NIV	68
6:3–8	141
6:11–14	117
6:15 NIV	117
6:23 NIV	62
6:33	16
7:9 NKJV	139
8:9 NKJV	116
8:9–11 ESV	67
8:17	149
8:22–25	70
8:29–30 NKJV	149
10:9 NIV	116
11	55
11:33	5
12:2	5
13:1	29
13:11	91
13:14	71
13:14 ESV	71
14:7 NKJV	111
14:9 NKJV	139
14:11	93, 149
15:4–6 NIV	152

1 Corinthians

1:18	126
3:2	153
3:17	61
6:2 ESV	146
10:1–2	101
10:11	85
11:30	91
13:12	5
14:33	70
15	60, 146
15:3–4	52
15:17–20 NKJV	111
15:18	28, 91
15:20	28
15:20–26	18
15:23	28
15:23 NLT	109
15:24	104, 151
15:24–26	131
15:25	142
15:26, 55	115

15:28	142
15:36	65
15:37	66
15:42–54 NIV	66–67
15:45	111
15:45–47 ESV	27
15:45–49	115
15:48–49 NIV	147
15:50 NIV	65
15:51 KJV	29
15:53	29
15:54	147
15:55	115

2 Corinthians

1:20	140
2:6	67
2:15	126
3:11, 13	85
3:13	85
4	69
4:3	126
4:7	67
4:16	70
5:1	70
5:1–2 NKJV	69
5:1–10	53
5:4	69, 70
5:8	72
5:8 KJV	57
5:9	72
5:10	58
5:10 NIV	128
5:17 ESV	67
5:21	33, 115
6:2	141
6:2 NLT	92
12:2, 4	105
12:4	105

Galatians

1:24	85
2:20	72
3:13	112
3:37 NIV	71
6:15 NLT	68

Index

Ephesians
2:4–6 ESV	97
2:12	55
2:19 NKJV	55
3:18 NLT	7
4:30	92
5:14	91

Philippians
1:6	3
1:21–22	57
1:23	53
1:23 NIV	57
1:28	61
2:10	93
2:10–11	149
2:12 NKJV	118
3:11	58
3:14	64
3:19	61
3:20–21	70
4:3	149

Colossians
1:22 NLT	97–98
1:26	85
1:27	98
2	120
2:3	120
2:12–13	141
3:2–4	72, 97
3:4	58
3:4 NLT	107
4	120

1 Thessalonians
	101, 102
4	60
4:7	64
4:14	58
4:15	100
4:16	72
4:16–17 NKJV	100
4:17	72
4:36	92
5:6	90
5:6–7, 10	91
5:9–10 NKJV	116
5:10	91

2 Thessalonians
1:6	73
1:6–7	137
1:7–9	73
1:7–10 NRSV	12
1:8 NIV	20
1:9	86
2:10	126

1 Timothy
2:5	147
2:5 KJV	111
6:16	28

2 Timothy
1:10 KJV	29
3:16	7
4:1 KJV	57, 58
4:7–8 KJV	58

Hebrews
	88
2:9	16
2:10	64
2:14	84
3:1 NLT	63
3:14 NKJV	65
4:15	28
4:16	97
5:7 NLT	33
5:11–12 NIV	153
7:14–18	85
8:13	8
9:27	17, 65, 133
9:28	57
10:11–14	18
10:17 NKJV	145
10:20–22	97
10:26–31 NIV	117
10:27 NIV	88
10:39	76
11	58

Index

11:5 NKJV	65
11:6	60
11:13	59
11:30–40 NIV	58
11:32	60
11:39	74
12:23	147
12:23 ESV, NKJV, NLT	150
12:25	64
12:29	87
13:6	83
13:8	8

James

1:5	5, 20
1:15	61
1:15 KJV	62
2:26	31
3:6	77
4:12	61
5:3, 5, 19	61
5:5	61
5:19	61
5:20	29
5:20 NIV	62

1 Peter

1:3, 23	68
1:3–4 NKJV	65
1:4–5	71
1:18–19	115
3:20	29
4:12 NIV	61
5:4	58

2 Peter

1:14–15 NIV	69
1:16–19 NLT	48
2:1 ESV	116
2:3 NIV	119
2:4–9	119
2:5	126
2:6	81
2:12 NIV	116
2:20–22	116–117

3	62
3:3–12 NIV	121
3:7	122
3:8	135
3:9	89
3:9 ESV	122
3:9 NIV	13
3:10	137
3:10–11 NIV	61
3:13	93
3:16 NIV	20

1 John

3:8 ESV	116
3:14–15 NKJV	62, 149
4:8	6
4:18	102
4:18 NIV	6

Jude

	117
7	95
7 ESV	81
7 NASB	81
7 NKJV	81, 87

Revelation

1, 76, 84, 120, 142

1:5	108
1:18	18, 51
2:7	146
2:10	58
2:10 NKJV	107
2:11	92
2:11–12	92
2:25–27	121, 146
3:5 ESV	148
3:10 NIV	106
3:21 NIV	146
4:4	97
5:9–10	121
5:10	146
5:12	112
6 KJV	73
6:9–10	73
6:9–11	53
7:2–3 ESV	106

Index

Revelation (*continued*)

7:9–17 NKJV	95–96
7:13–14 NKJV	106
7:15	96
9:4 ESV	106
9:5	84
11:10	84
11:18	106
11:18 NIV	62
12:5	104
12:17 ESV	107
13:5	135
13:7 ESV	107
13:8	112
13:10 NLT	106
13:15 NIV	107
14:10	125
14:10–11 NKJV	82
14:11	84
14:12	106
14:12 ESV	106
14:13	92
14:13 NIV	107
16:3 KJV	29
16:19	125
17:6	73
17:8	151
18:7, 10	84
18:8	82
18:9, 18	61
18:10	84
18:18	61
18:19	82
18:21	82
20	145
20:1–4 NASB	130
20:2–7	133
20:4	59
20:4 NASB	141
20:4–5 NASB	74
20:4–7 NKJV	138
20:5 NKJV	138
20:6	18, 58, 92, 121, 146
20:7	107, 120
20:7–8	131
20:12	146
20:12 NASB	144
20:13	18, 51
20:15	35
21	18, 96
21:2	59
21:2–3	18
21:2–4 NKJV	96
21:3 ESV	101
21:4	137
21:4 NKJV	11
21:6	97
21:27	144, 149
22:2	151
22:3	18, 94
22:4	137
22:17 NIV	64

www.ingramcontent.com/pod-product-compliance
Lightning Source LLC
Chambersburg PA
CBHW050817160426
43192CB00010B/1793